Politics, Religion, and the Common Good

Advancing a Distinctly American Conversation About Religion's Role in Our Shared Life

Martin E. Marty with
Jonathan Moore

Jossey-Bass Publishers
San Francisco

Jossey-Bass books and products are available through most bookstores. To contact Jossey-Bass directly, call (888) 378-2537, fax to (800) 605-2665, or visit our Website at www.josseybass.com.

Substantial discounts on bulk quantities of Jossey-Bass books are available to corporations, professional associations, and other organizations. For details and discount information, contact the special sales department at Jossey-Bass.

 Manufactured in the United States of America on Lyons Falls Turin Book. This paper is acid-free and 100 percent chlorine-free.

Library of Congress Cataloging-in-Publication Data

Marty, Martin E., date
    Politics, religion, and the common good : advancing a distinctly
American conversation about religion's role in our shared life / Martin E. Marty
with Jonathan Moore.— 1st ed.
      p. cm.
    Includes bibliographical references and index.
    ISBN 0-7879-5031-9 (alk. paper)
    1. Religion and politics—United States. 2. United States—Religion.
I. Moore, Jonathan, date II. Title.
BL2525 .M375 2000
322'.1'0973—dc21   99-50450

FIRST EDITION
HB Printing 10 9 8 7 6 5 4 3 2 1

Contents

Politics, Religion, and the Common Good

Introduction:
Tools for Moving from
Argument to Conversation

On September 11, 1998, a curious event occurred at the White House. The president convoked an unusual gathering of highly visible clergy to the usual Religious Leaders' Breakfast. There he confessed that he had sinned and asked for the forgiveness of all the American people.

In what other republic or industrialized nation would the chief executive or prime minister regard himself as a sort of priest who could convoke clergy and then turn himself into a penitent, turning the American people, as a body, into confessors?

None.

United States citizens, with few alert, noisy, and scrupulous exceptions, take such actions for granted. At any moment, half of them may not like the way a particular president plays priest and pastor. Liking or not liking depends in part on the political taste of critics and fans. It depends in part how they read the First Amendment to the United States Constitution and how careful they are about drawing a line between religion and civil authority or how messy they choose to be about lines that almost inevitably blur.

Reaction to the 1998 Religious Leaders' Breakfast revealed, if nothing else did, how the American people were ending the decade, the century, and the millennium, showing with good reason that they remain confused about the ways religion relates to government and the way politics gets webbed with religion.

You would think that in the more than two centuries since the American colonists got rid of the king and the American constitutionalists set the priests aside from their government, the people and their leaders would have sorted out the various roles religious figures do and should play in national life. They have not. Confusion keeps growing.

In an effort to help readers make sense of the events of 1998, political scientist Sebastian de Grazia, author of *A Country with No Name: Tales from the Constitution,* traced the confusion through history.[1] He asked whether the president's convoking and confessing showed him to be "high priest, ecumenical patriarch, archbishop, pontifex maximus." Keeping the incident in mind, de Grazia asked, "Was this unheard-of appeal to the American people an idiosyncrasy of the incumbent president, a presidential act unlikely to ever occur again, or does it have broader implications?"

It has broader implications.

The Constitution, reminded de Grazia, "did not contemplate the President's becoming a religious or spiritual leader. The Constitution made no mention of God." Yet moral leaders such as Washington, Lincoln, Wilson, and Franklin Delano Roosevelt attached God to their exhortations. Jefferson resisted the priestly role. The Constitution, he thought, prohibited the government "from meddling with religious institutions, their doctrines, disciplines, or exercises." Until the 1950s, presidents violated Jefferson's definition only in wartime and only then assuming the priestly role to rally a religion-favoring populace.

Then came Dwight Eisenhower, who became "convinced that his mission as President was to restore the nation's spirituality." He himself was baptized the Sunday after he was inaugurated. Soon Congress inserted the words "under God" into the Pledge of Allegiance, which public schoolchildren were expected to recite daily. Eisenhower started the presidential prayer breakfast tradition that any subsequent president would disrupt at peril to his or her reputation.

Each subsequent president has had his own style, but every one has felt called upon to identify himself as a professing Christian. The most recent have identified themselves as born-again Christians and each of these has tended to embody one or more of the following traits: "evangelism, a preacherly rhetoric, the baptism of believers, a crusading zeal, and reliance on the Book."

Again one asks, where else would the top officer of government aspire to anything like this, and where else would the people accept it or, indeed, not rise up against it?

The September 11 incident, in de Grazia's eyes, was peculiar also for what it revealed to other nations about Americans' self-description: "They have locked in a materialist stereotype the country [the President] presides over." And "somehow the globe today appears not to see America bathed in the . . . spiritual light" that had Americans in their own eyes assuming moral leadership. Therefore, "when countries religiously estranged from the United States look for some sign of spirituality, there is generally not much visible to the naked eye. They have little choice but to look to the President."

Meanwhile, de Grazia urged, there is likely to be in future decades "a certain amount of competition among clergy for the President's favor," and "the President will take on more and more openly the colouring of a high priest" as "the presidential ecumene [spiritually interactive worlds] seems to be expanding." No serious presidential candidate can be elected if not at home in that "ecumene."

Closer to Home: Issues of Politics and Religion

Despite all the media attention, the September 11, 1998, event is far from the personal experience of most citizens. If they favor a president and his or her convoked clergy, they will applaud the priestly role of this civil authority. If they disfavor a president and the set of clergy he or she favors, they will be critical of all—and then wait for their kind of president to invite their kind of clergy for the kind of priestly ceremonies they like. Still, it all seems remote.

Close to home, however, all citizens, whether they know it or show it, are involved in these unsettled understandings of government, politics, and religion.

For example, suppose you are a taxpaying property owner in a residential suburb that thrives chiefly on homeowners' taxes. You are religiously indifferent, perhaps a bit hostile to organized religion, and you are surrounded by churches you despise. And they do not pay property taxes, which means that your taxes are somewhat higher and you indirectly subsidize them and their doings. Is that fair? Advisable? Constitutional?

Or you are a taxpaying property owner who helps subsidize public school education. You may have withdrawn your children from the public schools because you disagree with some school practices and teachings. You and your spouse work outside the home and cannot sustain home schooling. Thus you must send your children to religiously run schools that charge tuition. "We're getting double-taxed," you'll say.

Or you may agree with what the public school is about but have a religious commitment that leads you to want your children to become responsible citizens through parochial education. You get no financial relief for having taken some of the burden off the public school and thus having lowered its expenses. Is that fair? Advisable? Constitutional?

You may not have the luxury of belonging to a communion that quarrels little with mainstream ways of doing things. If you are a Christian Scientist and thus a disbeliever in conventional medicine or a Jehovah's Witness and therefore object to blood transfusions, you might see the civil courts reach in and take your children from you temporarily while they get standard medical care of sorts that violate your religious commitment. God gave you those children. The government takes them away, you say. Is that fair? Advisable?

You are assured the "free exercise of religion" by the First Amendment to the Constitution. Yet you are not free to exercise *your* religion in public places on the public's time. You cannot have the Ten Commandments on the courtroom wall, prescribed Bible reading or prayer in the public classroom, or your version of creation taught in the schools while other moral frameworks, philosophies, and what look to you like religions get a free ride. Is that fair? Advisable?

In political campaigns, you are an economic conservative who also supports abortion and gay rights. Yet you know that no candidate can be chosen to represent your party unless he or she caters to Christian conservative coalitions that militate against your stand. Or you are a pro-life citizen who resents the fact that in order to get elected, your candidate wavers on the religiously inspired social issues. Why must you tolerate such cruel alternatives within your party?

Or you are a liberal, and you ground your convictions about government and politics in divine law, natural law, the words of the prophets and mystics, and the spiritual leaders of your tradition. You are not so much nonreligious as "other-religious." Yet the questions that poll takers ask and the reports in the newspapers tend to categorize you as unmoved by religion just because you don't follow the style of religiosity they instantly recognize. Why can't you rely on your distinctive religious coloring in politics?

Far from the White House, in your house, issues like these present themselves every day.

The Need to Think and Converse About These Issues

It may have seemed insulting to read that Americans remain "confused" about how government and politics interact with religion. Most intense and partisan activists will say they are not confused. They are perfectly clear about walls of separation between church and state and whether someone is violating them. They know exactly what it means that "Congress shall make no law respecting an establishment of religion" and that they are to have free exercise of religion. It's someone else who is confused and spreads confusion to the point that you get frustrated, furious, left out. Then you meet someone else who bullies you into a corner with an argument you find hard to refute. You have never had to think deeply about these things. Now you scramble to stay ahead.

Put the title "member of the board" before a name, and it is likely that you will enter the company of the confused. Be a member of the school board, hospital board, library board, zoning board, town board, church trustees board, or community college board, and you'll likely see incidents that erupt routinely, problems that constantly appear. You and your colleagues gather the whole board and invite the whole public. In the resulting conversation, you do not want to miss an opportunity on the one hand or get assaulted by those who stir these issues on the other. You need a resource on which to draw, a framework to do your own thinking, a sense of what has gone on elsewhere. We hope this book will be one such resource.

You want to do the right thing by your God, your tradition, your country, the public order, the law and the courts, and your fellow citizens. You have found that shouting, polarization, and demeaning arguments are of no help. We hope that the model of conversation presented in this book will be helpful.

The Basics: Politics, Religion, and Public Religion

To encourage conversation about religion and politics, we think it's important for every person to have some basic tools in his or her citizenship toolbox. The elemental tools—the hammer and nails—for our project are clear understandings of what we're talking about. What do we mean by *politics*? By *religion*? By *public religion*?

Politics

To stimulate your imagination, let's look at some of the pithy and provocative things that cynical, humorous, and thoughtful people have said politics is:[2]

> "The art of the next best." (Otto von Bismarck)
>
> "A realm, peopled only by villains or heroes, in which everything is black or white and gray is a forbidden color." (John Mason Brown)
>
> "The moral man's compromise, the swindler's method, and the fool's hope." (John Ciardi)
>
> "The possession and distribution of power." (Benjamin Disraeli)
>
> "Persuading the public to vote for this and support that and endure these for the promise of those." (Gilbert Highet)
>
> "The most interesting thing you can do." (John F. Kennedy)
>
> "An activity in which the choice is constantly between two evils." (John Morley)
>
> "A profession in which you cannot be true to all your friends all of the time." (Michael Pazaine)
>
> "The art of making possible that which is necessary." (Paul Valéry)

In a slightly more sustained fashion, British political scientist Bernard Crick provides a rich description of the meaning and function of politics in a republic:

> Politics is conservative—it preserves the minimum benefits of established order; politics is liberal—it is compounded of particular liberties and it requires tolerance; politics is socialist—it provides conditions for deliberate

social change by which groups can come to feel that they have an equitable stake in the prosperity and survival of the community. . . . Politics does not just hold the fort; it creates a thriving and polyglot community outside the castle walls.

Politics . . . is a way of ruling in divided societies without undue violence. This is both to assert, historically, that there are some societies at least which contain a variety of different interests and differing moral viewpoints; and to assert, ethically, that conciliation is at least to be preferred to coercion among normal people. . . . Political ethics are not some inferior type of ethical activity, but are a level of ethical life fully self-contained and fully justifiable. Politics is not just a necessary evil; it is a realistic good.

Political activity is a type of moral activity; it is free activity, and it is inventive, flexible, enjoyable, and human; it can create some sense of community and yet is not, for instance, a slave to nationalism; it does not claim to settle every problem or to make every sad heart glad, but it can help some way in nearly everything and, where it is strong, it can prevent the vast cruelties and deceits of ideological rule.[3]

Religion

For some people, religion means everything listed in the "Churches and Synagogues" section of the Yellow Pages. For others, religion means the individualized spirituality so popular today. People may also include various forms of public or civil religion, some of them connected with the state itself. Sociologist Peter Berger has spoken of a "sacred canopy" that arches over individual life and that of subcommunities.[4] What goes on under this sacred canopy is part of our concern when discussing religion and politics.

Before we get into the scholarly understandings, I wish again to provoke your imagination, stimulate discussion, entertain, and illustrate the wide range of possibilities, this time exploring definitions of religion:[5]

"The search for a value underlying all things." (Gordon W. Allport)

"The voice of the deepest human experience." (Matthew Arnold)

"Man's search . . . for strength and courage to be gained from the heart of spiritual matter, greater than an individual man, greater than the more or less human race." (Bernard Iddings Bell)

"A phase of a people's total interaction with the objective world of nature, organized society and the accumulated tradition of an historic past." (William C. Bower)

"The basis of civil society, and the source of all good and all comfort." (Edmund Burke)

"The holy service of God." (William Camden)

"The sense of ultimate reality, of whatever meaning a man finds in his own existence or the existence of anything else." (G. K. Chesterton)

"The rule of life, not a casual incident of it." (Benjamin Disraeli)

"A bandage that man has invented to protect a soul made bloody by circumstance." (Theodore Dreiser)

"The emotion of reverence which the presence of the universal mind ever excites in the individual." (Ralph Waldo Emerson)

"A universal obsessional neurosis." (Sigmund Freud)

"The feelings, acts, and experiences of individual men in their solitude, so far as they apprehend themselves to stand in relation to whatever they may consider the divine." (William James)

"A sense of something transcending the expected or natural." (Robert C. Lowie)

"The opium of the people." (Karl Marx)

"A noble attempt to suggest in human terms more-than-human realities." (Christopher Morley)

"The idea of a Moral Governor, and a particular Providence." (John Henry Newman)

"Man's attempt to get in touch with an absolute spiritual Reality behind the phenomena of the Universe, and having made contact with It, to live in harmony with It." (Arnold J. Toynbee)

Now for a more sustained effort. Scholars will never agree on the definition of religion, but here we consider five features that can help point to and put boundaries around the term.

1. Religion Focuses Our "Ultimate Concern"

Religion focuses for the faithful what theologian Paul Tillich called their "ultimate concern."[6] What is the overarching purpose of life? What do we most care about? For what would you be willing to die? Citizens can answer those questions in many different ways—and sometimes in ways that go beyond what we typically think is "religious." For example, if one is willing to die for the ideas symbolized by the swastika, that points toward an "ultimate concern." If one believes not that the universe is related to a deity but instead that human fate depends on the location of the stars at the time of one's birth, that faith points to an astrological ultimate concern for the starred person. Those who think that "I" connects with "It" as an energy field pervading the universe and who order their lives around this thought have found their object of ultimate concern in something today coded as "New Age," even if they are on the church rolls as Catholic or Episcopalian. Tillich's notion of ultimate concern allows us to consider "religious" any belief systems that take up the meaning and purpose of human existence.

Ultimate concern, because it points to the very meaning of life itself, naturally has something to do with politics and government. Politics asks many questions that can either further or hinder one's understanding of ultimate concern. How should society be ordered? What is society's responsibility to the poor? How much money should we spend on the military? Should abortion or assisted suicide be legal? How much control should the state have over family life? Politics and government must answer these questions, and in doing so they must consider the multiple and often contradictory ultimate concerns of its citizens. And citizens, in helping shape political answers to those questions, will unavoidably rely on their ultimate concerns in making decisions. The intermingling of religion—understood as ultimate concern—and politics is therefore inescapable.

2. Religion Builds Community

Ultimate concern does not by itself point to religion, as religion is traditionally understood; the phrase is too broad to identify the subset of overarching commitments that we usually call "religious." Another element of religion is the impulse to build community, to form social responses.

"Take the shoes off your feet, for the ground on which you are standing is holy" (Exodus 3:5): this word to Moses from a voice near a burning bush that was not consumed is followed immediately with a call to find and deal with and lead what the voice calls "my people." The creator of awe wants a religious people of a special sort to be formed as a people, a social order, a community. Though in late modern times, individualized religion has become increasingly popular, social forms of religion still overwhelmingly predominate.

Religion's impulse to community has rich and obvious implications for politics. Most people who enter political life do it as part of a mission, and some feel called to live a life of public service as part of a religious duty. Even those driven chiefly by self-interest must convince an electorate that they have in mind broader concerns for justice, equity, and the general welfare. A politician's constituents, at all levels of government, will normally belong to multiple communities, including religious groups. Successful politicians will need to attend to the perspectives of those communities if they hope to remain in office.

3. Religion Appeals to Myth and Symbol

The religious do more than engage in rational, matter-of-fact discourse about public matters. Indeed, religious adherents are often motivated by myth and symbol. Myth, in this context, does not point to something fictional or untrue; instead, myth refers to extraordinary means of stating truths. For those who respond, myth is often the only way to fully capture truth, and such myths help organize communities. Thus the scriptural "I will be your God and you will be my people" does better than "we the people of the United States" for purposes of building religious community. "In the beginning, God created the heavens and the earth" and "the human is made in the image of God" are claims that better reorient group life than mathematical renderings of the Big Bang or evolutionary explanations of human origins do. The political rhetorician who has to summon the energies of a demoralized people and propel them into action will not say "Eighty-seven years ago some colonists declared independence from their colonizers" but rather "Fourscore and seven years ago, our fathers brought forth a new nation."

As with myth, so with symbol. The Star of David, the Crescent, the Cross, the sacred meal, the rite of initiation—all symbolize the "special and surprising" messages of particular faiths. Other systems of ultimate concern also appeal to symbols—the swastika, the fasces, the rising sun, the hammer and sickle all point toward comprehensive understandings of reality and human purpose.

The religious appeal to myth and symbol affects politics in obvious ways. Politics often mimics this appeal—politicians and citizens alike respond to mythical stories, and government often evokes many kinds of symbols. Whoever has been to the Tomb of the Unknown Soldier or the Vietnam War Memorial in Washington, D.C.; whoever has heard debates over the need for a constitutional amendment prohibiting flag burning; whoever has known the terrifying power of the Ku Klux Klan insignia or America Nazi Party emblems; whoever has read the speeches of Abraham Lincoln—all are aware of the emotive, bonding, and impelling power of stories that come as myth and signs that come as symbols.

4. Religion Is Reinforced Through Rites and Ceremonies

Religion includes the impulse to reinforce religious faith through rites and ceremonies. Male children might be circumcised, community members might be baptized, or converts may make an official pledge. Other rites greet the new spring, plead for a prosperous planting and harvest, bind couples in marriage, or prepare individuals for death. The profound and awe-inspiring religions point toward "another world" by using rites and ceremonies to invest "ordinary" events with greater significance.

Politics also depends on rites and ceremonies. They include such activities as administering an oath of office, swearing in new citizens, and publicly commemorating important historical events. Even in avowedly secular nations, such as those once behind the Iron Curtain, leaders depend on rites and ceremonies to foster group identity. Rites and ceremonies help a group of people form and remain a coherent community.

5. Religion Demands Certain Behaviors from Its Adherents

Almost all religions stipulate that followers behave in certain ways and not in others. The potent religions also stipulate behavioral correlates and consequences for adherents. From the vital faiths come various demands: You must attend Mass. You mustn't drink intoxicating beverages. You must refrain from eating pork. You must make a pilgrimage to Mecca. You must place joss sticks on the sacred fire at the dawn of the new year. The more religion expects and exacts such behaviors, the more adherents will draw a distinctive boundary between themselves and others.

Politics and governments also demand certain behaviors. Politicians pass laws, and governments enforce them; citizens can expect to be penalized if they don't follow society's rules. Citizens who transgress certain rules may be accused of treason—the political form of heresy.

Public Religion

Americans often speak of religion as "a private affair." Yet as long ago as 1749, Benjamin Franklin spoke of "the necessity of a publick religion" for the health of the republic.[7] We contend that America still needs "publick religion," which has much to contribute to the common good. But what do we mean by *public religion*?

As with the term *religion*, we forgo a precise definition and instead point to phenomena that help describe what we're talking about. This first thing to notice is that *public* religion is naturally posed against *private* religion. But is this polarity helpful?

In some senses, public religion can only be understood in opposition to private religion: public religion is what private religion is not, and vice versa. But this polarity can often restrict our vision. Some scholars have suggested that these two categories do not exhaust the possibilities; for example, a concept like "the social" can help describe places where public and private intersect.

Public and private need not refer to polar opposites. Public religion would not exist were there not repositories of private faith in the consciousness and practice of millions of Americans. And such so-called private religion depends in many ways on the public legal framework and cultural environment in which faiths prosper.

There are clearly many reasons to use the term *public religion* with care, but we still think it is a useful concept. For us, public religion refers to religion's public implications, those places where religion seems to have an identifiable—and potentially extricable—influence on public life.

When and Where to Talk:
Some Settings for Dialogue

As we have seen, public religion and politics share many features. Indeed, it is hard to think of any descriptions, definitions, or citations of profound elements in politics and government that are not somehow religious. As well, public religion and politics inevitably intersect. With some basic tools in hand, we now turn to the interactions between religion and politics and how best to negotiate those interactions.

When and where should we talk? Whenever and wherever people discuss politics. Politics, by dealing with proposals for the common good, inevitably touches on people's basic ideas about what is most important in life. For most Americans, this means drawing on religious understandings of reality and human purpose. Here are some more specific occasions where this kind of dialogue can and should occur:

Whenever individuals seek greater personal understanding of how religion and politics interact, so as to better enable informed and active citizenship

Where individuals—whether as voters, activists, or leaders—find opportunities to act publicly for the civic good

Whenever school boards, library boards, hospital boards, church groups, or other community organizations face creative or disruptive challenges involving the public good

In adult education courses or college classes that touch on religion and politics

Where public policymakers, philanthropic foundations, or corporations don't want to be caught off guard by sudden changes on the religion-and-politics front

How to Talk: Argument, Conversation, and Dialogue

If this book is to advance a national conversation, we should be clear about what we mean by *conversation*. What is real conversation? Is it any different from *argument* or *dialogue*? These words have rich possibilities and are worth discussing.

Should We Argue?

"Civilization is formed by men locked together in argument," observed the Dominican priest Thomas Gilbey.[8] In *argument*, the various sides propose theses and then set out to make a point. Serious arguers propose theses as truths and then insist that their truths are the correct answers to the problem. Thus I can defend the thesis that since the Constitution assures "free exercise of religion," this free exercise must mean that teachers have a right to conduct classroom devotions in line with their beliefs and those of the majority of pupils. You can argue that such devotions and neglect of the minority are contrary to the "establishment of religion" clause. We read the history of the Constitution, study law and history, summon logic, figuratively roll up our sleeves and engage one another. If as contestants we cannot convert those on the other side to our truth, we will want at least to defeat them. By conversion or mere victory, we hope to demonstrate that we, and not our opponents, have the more persuasive position.

Father John Courtney Murray, one of the great theorists of republican existence, placed argument at the center of his understanding of America. Drawing on the insight of Thomas Gilbey, Murray proposed that "the distinctive bond of the civil multitude is reason, or more exactly, that exercise of reason which is argument."[9] Without civil argument, citizens and their representatives could not legislate in ways that might ensure some measure of justice or equity. Self-interested people make up the body politic, and their desires are not shared by others. Politics thrives on argument between these various interests. Government, or at least good government, results when these interests successfully address the common good.

But what is the American argument about? In an important 1960 work, Murray developed an answer to that question. For Murray, the American argument concerned three major themes. First, "the argument is about public affairs, the *res publica*, those matters which are for the advantage of the public (in the phrase as old as Plato) and which call for public decision and action by government." Second, the American argument "concerns the affairs of the commonwealth." And finally, "the most important and the most difficult" theme of the American argument "concerns the constitutional consensus whereby the people acquires its identity as a people and the society is endowed with its vital form, . . . its sense of purpose as a collectivity organized for action in history."[10]

What does Murray mean by this consensus? "This consensus is come to by the people; they become a people by coming to it. . . . It is an ensemble of substantive truths, a structure of basic knowledge, an order of elementary affirmations that reflect realities inherent in the order of existence." Murray contended that "the whole premise of the public argument, if it is to be civilized and civilizing, is that the consensus is real, that among the people everything is not in doubt, but that there is a core of agreement, accord, concurrence, acquiescence. We hold certain truths; therefore we can argue about them."[11]

For all its virtues and potential, argument also has limits. Too often arguments are unfairly tilted toward the side with a better social position, more economic privileges, or a better education. In political argument, well-financed lobbies exert power far beyond the numbers of people they represent. To take a controversial example, polls say that the public has for years favored many kinds of gun control. But the National Rifle Association, representing a highly dedicated minority of citizens, can focus and provide its resources and energies to help ensure the election of candidates who will speak up for policies the NRA favors. By the time a legislature has been elected, the candidates favoring one approach may well be in position to command the media, to summon arguments—and to keep the underorganized majority at a distance.

Another example: higher education empowers its graduates to use logic, rhetoric, research, and the prestige of the master's degree to counter and overwhelm those with only eighth-grade educations from underfunded inner-city schools. Those with the graduate education have their own interests to protect, their own goals to meet, their own patrons and employers to satisfy, their own politicians to enthrall. They may not argue as well from the heart as the victims of bad public education would, but the former will outargue the latter by the rules of the game in American political life.

Women have long made the case that at least until recently, men held positions, brought experience, and could draw on past cases to outargue women who were denied such positions and opportunities. As women gained more employment outside the home, more experience in the working world, and more higher education, their arguments improved significantly, and they won more.

In those three examples, there had to be a winner. And the winner was determined by who could buy the most votes, sell the most policies, and determine the favored approaches to living.

Argument can take forms that, at the expense of the weak, merely guarantee more power to the powerful. Seeking to convince, convert, or defeat others, arguments often serve simply to humiliate, silence, or exclude. We have all seen attorneys, either in person or on television, staying within the rules of the game—a good judge will enforce that—and yet using experience, license, and convention to bully poor, undereducated, inarticulate victims of abuse who seek a forum for justice in the light of their complaints.

Sometimes argument bogs down midcourse; opponents weary of fighting but are no closer to closure. This results in resentful publics and unmet problems. This kind of thing we have seen in the prolonged legislative debates over abortion policies. The legislators and the public cannot avoid argument. Abortion rights and limits to abortion have to be settled by law, and lawmakers have to be convinced by lobbyists or convince each other. Yet they can stalemate, and few try to think of fresh approaches to social problems related to abortion or its prohibition.

Upon reaching a stalemate, both sides can "agree to disagree" on one subject so that they can move on and deal with other matters, or they may simply retreat to permanent warring camps. Either way, the argument remains unresolved, and progress toward the common good screeches to a halt.

On many contemporary issues, Americans find that their arguments have led to unbudgeable roadblocks. Publics are indeed "locked" together in argument, but not the civil kind envisioned by Father Murray. Instead, publics are at loggerheads, locked into alienating positions, unable to convert or defeat opponents and left to shout contending truths at one another. If a republic cannot thrive without argument, it clearly cannot thrive on argument alone.

Let's Have a Conversation

A conversation, wrote theologian David Tracy, "is not a confrontation. It is not a debate. It is not an exam. It is questioning itself. It is a willingness to follow the question wherever it may go."[12] Although argument often unfairly privileges certain sides over others, true *conversation* is more likely to occur between equals. If the nature of argument is determined by competing truth propositions, the character of conversation is determined by the questions asked. David Tracy has much to teach us about conversation. In *Pluralism and Ambiguity,* he explains that "the movement in conversation is questioning itself. Neither my present opinions on the question nor the . . . original response to the question, but the question itself, must control every conversation."[13]

Tracy has much more to say on the nature of conversation. It is "a game," he says, "with some hard rules: say only what you mean; say it as accurately as you can; listen to and respect what the other says, however different or other; be willing to correct or defend your opinions if challenged by the conversation partner; be willing to argue if necessary, to confront if demanded, to endure necessary conflict, to change your mind if the evidence suggests it."[14]

Conversation takes on the character of a game and relies on surprise and on unexpected insights and unanticipated resources from the other side. Conversation encourages risk, allows for experiment, and promises fresh angles of vision. A civil order, we believe, needs much more than argument. America can prosper only if citizens learn to participate in conversation with one another.

Now That We're Talking, What Are We Talking About?

This book makes several claims about religion and American political life. Readers, of course, can agree or disagree with them and leave it at that. But rather than merely accepting or rejecting our argument, we hope you will read this book as a sincere invitation to conversation. We offer the following theses to stimulate conversation, and we expect—and welcome—agreement and disagreement alike.

1. Public religion can be dangerous; it should be handled with care.

2. Public religion can and does contribute to the common good.

3. Individual citizens energized by an awareness of possibilities based on their beliefs and the effects of those beliefs provide hope for improving the republic.

4. Traditional institutions—congregations, denominations, and ecumenical agencies—provide an effective public voice for religious people, but the political power of such groups has declined.

5. For the foreseeable future, religious people will most commonly funnel their political energies into special-interest groups, voluntary associations, and parachurch organizations.

6. It is important for the common good for religious people to join the political conversation—and get involved.

In the chapters in this book, we will explain these points in greater depth. The chapters of this book report on and derive from several formal conversations on a variety of themes related to politics and religion. Some themes were brought up at more than one of the consultations. Thus, to inspire study and conversation in the different kinds of groups that will be drawn to discuss the separate chapters, those issues and motifs also appear in more than one chapter here. Let the conversation begin!

Handle with Care
The Case Against Public Religion

*Thesis: Public religion can be dangerous; it should be
handled with care.*

In the 1940s, what could incite otherwise law-abiding white Christian Americans to treat a group of fellow white Christian citizens like this?

In Nebraska, one member of this group was castrated.

In Wyoming, another member was tarred and feathered.

In Maine, six members were reportedly beaten.

In Illinois, a caravan of group members was attacked.

In other states, sheriffs looked the other way as people assaulted group members.

The group's meeting places were also attacked.

Members of the group were commonly arrested and then imprisoned without being charged.

Certainly the castrated, tarred, beaten, attacked, imprisoned people must have posed a great threat to the republic to prompt such behavior. They must have been revolutionaries whose ideologies led them to plot the overthrow of government by violent means. Who were they? Communists? Nazis? Anarchists?

They were Jehovah's Witnesses. One would expect that the law of the land, as interpreted by the Supreme Court, would have protected them. After all, we are talking about the middle of the twentieth century, more than one hundred fifty years after the Constitution had assured religious freedom and equal protection under law.

Yet in 1940 the Court did just the opposite: it ruled against a religious practice of an essentially peaceful people.

What had the Jehovah's Witnesses done? They had circulated pamphlets such as "Reasons Why a True Follower of Jesus Christ Cannot Salute a Flag." According to their strict interpretation of Exodus 20:3–5, not saluting the U.S. flag was as sacred to Jehovah's Witnesses as honoring the flag was to the American majority.

With war beginning to rage in Europe and threatening to involve the United States, the pamphlets—and thus the Jehovah's Witnesses, already known for disdaining civic obligations—were interpreted as unpatriotic. The country had to stand together. Schoolchildren were forced to salute the flag by an action of the Supreme Court. But the Jehovah's Witnesses didn't go along with this. To them, the flag was an icon, an idol, a symbol of an authority other than God. (In 1935, official Jehovah's Witness literature argued that saluting the flag was a U.S. import of the Nazi "Heil Hitler!" salute and noted that Hitler was persecuting their fellow believers in Germany.)

Within three years, there was a happy ending for all but those who *did* want the salute forced and enforced. The Court majority reversed itself. But during the three years before that reversal, it became obvious that religion, which can pose "us" versus "them"—or "them" versus what we think "the state" should be and do—carries risks and can be perceived by others as dangerous.

Religion can cause all kinds of trouble in the public arena. The world scene reveals many instances of terror and tragedy created by people acting in the name of religion. Late-twentieth-century wars often involved religiously motivated belligerents invoking sacred powers to justify horrible acts. Mere place names evoke tragedies where religion plays a central role: Northern Ireland, Afghanistan, the West Bank, East Timor, Yugoslavia. It matters little which religion is involved; blood has been spilled by devotees of most faith traditions. Single-minded and impassioned, religious people often feel chosen by their God to work out the divine will against unbelievers—by any means necessary.

What about the scene closer to home?

Pro-choice people point to examples when pro-life individuals or groups inconvenience, harass, or even kill abortion providers in the name of God. Some religious groups blame religions they consider "false" as bearing responsibility for declines in morality and traditional family life.

Critics of religious groups that promote gay and lesbian marriage and fight for homosexual rights consider those groups—and their religion—dangerous because they call down or claim God's blessings for what the critics think are abhorrent and destructive actions. On the other side, liberal Christians point out that conservative biblical interpretation denies gays and lesbians their full humanity.

Religion inspires Native American activists to make claims on lands that once were theirs, claims that inconvenience nearby non-Indian farmers. Conflict overseas that is justified or inspired by religion and that involves kin of American population elements—in Northern Ireland, Serbia, Iran—stirs passions and can disrupt community in the United States. The charismatic head of the Nation of Islam speaks incendiary anti-Jewish denunciations in Madison Square Garden, and the rest of America gasps at such language coming from a religious leader.

What goes on here and in such cases?

Religion Divides

Those called to be religious naturally form separate groups, movements, tribes, or nations. Responding in good faith to a divine call, believers feel themselves endowed with sacred privilege, a sense of chosenness that elevates them above all others. This self-perception then leads groups to draw lines around themselves and to speak negatively of "the others." Thus Israel had its Canaan, Christianity its Jews and heathen, and Islam its infidels. The elect denounce "others" for worshiping false gods and often act violently against such unbelievers.

American history offers a long list of people who have claimed such sacred privilege for themselves—and for the nation as a whole. Massachusetts Bay Colony leader John Winthrop indicated this sense of elevated status when he told his fellow colonists, "We must consider that we shall be as a City upon a Hill, the eyes of all people are upon us." Others since Winthrop have sung of the United States as "God's New Israel."[1] Ronald Reagan helped draw a similar boundary when he spoke of the Soviet Union as an "evil empire." American leaders and those they represent have often claimed special status for the United States, speaking of the country as possessing a divinely chosen identity that places it above all others in relation to God's plan.

Religion Disrupts

Religious citizens do not necessarily improve community life when they justify their actions on spiritual grounds. As noted, some features of religion can tempt people to claim a monopoly on God or on knowledge of God's will—at the expense of the claims and knowledge of others. While religions claim to be resources for healing and reconciling people, they often serve as salt in old wounds or abrasions that cause new ones in the midst of community life.

Many of the nation's founders, well aware of religion's disruptive potential, worried that officially encouraging religion would only increase the chances for such trouble. Although some colonies had established churches, the new national compact avoided formal links between the state and religion. Such a linkage, constitutional father James Madison believed, would produce "knaves, hypocrites, and fools." "Knaves" would willfully exploit the power of religion to dominate the public masses, "hypocrites" would pretend that their personal faith matched the prejudices of larger publics, and "fools" might misunderstand the nature and power of religion and come across as inauthentic.

Steadfastly religious members of the founding generation similarly advised that religion and state should be kept separate. Baptist clergyman and founding father Isaac Backus believed that both religion and the state would be better off if kept separate from each other. "No man can be made a member of a truly religious society by force, or without his own consent," Backus contended, and "neither can any corporation that is not a religious society have a just right to govern in religious affairs."[2]

America has become more plural in its third century. Thus the introduction of religion into political matters runs an even greater risk of causing trouble. Think for a minute of the seemingly intractable, always contentious arguments over abortion. There religion often seems to do more to intensify passions than achieve resolution. Similarly, religion's divisiveness in the public sphere can be seen clearly when considering an issue such as homosexuality. Alan Wolfe has shown that even as Americans have grown more and more tolerant of each other, religious beliefs contribute to "a seemingly unbridgeable gulf . . . between those who believe that the Bible's condemnation of homosexuality as an abomination must be taken as a moral injunction versus those who believe that Christianity requires the love and acceptance of everyone."[3] At times, religion seems to do more to maintain and fortify political divisions than to heal them.

Religion Can Be Violent

"Violence is authorized by religion because religion is inherently absolutist in the type of authoritative claims it makes and in the all-encompassing nature of its demands on its followers," wrote Brian K.

Smith.[4] Once a particular group considers itself as divinely chosen
and draws sharp boundaries between itself and others, the enemy
has been clearly identified, and violence can become actual. Religion possesses special power for creating violence because its texts
and injunctions have ways of locating eternal, supernatural, and absolutist impulses in the temporal world or the natural order. Other
notions then follow.

To begin at the bottom, the Ku Klux Klan, both in its nineteenth-
century antiblack forms and in its twentieth-century anti-Jewish,
anti-Catholic expressions, was a base form of religion. Protestant
clergy who replaced pulpit garb with Klan robes and exchanged the
cross from their church with the burning cross on the lawn of
African Americans did so invoking the Bible on their own altar.

Militia members, bombers, white supremacists, and their ilk pick
up themes from scriptures, isolate them, and then treat them inde-
pendently of the nonviolent and peacemaking texts to justify subversive activities.

In the eyes of many, the readiness of the clergy to bless the can-
non in whatever war the United States is fighting (and there are
texts aplenty for this blessing) is a sign that faith communities have
no questions about armament, war, and the killing of people in
"evil" places—even, and often, against the counsel of fellow believers who accent other biblical themes.

Many an adult who feels deprived of childhood, who never had
an opportunity to make up his or her mind, blames religion for verbal or physical abuse: religion at its worst. And family members of
those who died at Jonestown or Waco have a ready answer to anyone who asks whether religion can produce violence.

Native Americans see a certain lake or tree to be sacred and set
out to protect it. But now it "belongs" to someone else, and that
someone, invoking his own God, perpetrates violence and is met
by counterviolence. A place comes to be seen as sacred, and the
people must engage in a crusade to take it from the infidel. Or this
particular time is pregnant, and a nation must use it to expand its

borders. Or this cause is unique, and a tribe must follow it and engage in ethnic cleansing. Religion in its intense forms can grasp people who would otherwise have multiple commitments and exact complete and exclusive expressions of their loyalty, "even unto death."

Many critics argue that violence is the logical end of *all* religious faith. Some critics say that religion's tendency to turn violent is especially true of monotheistic faiths—Judaism, Christianity, Islam. Because by nature they invoke an exclusivist, jealous God, monotheistic religions cannot avoid perpetrating violence against those outside the faith. Regina M. Schwarz offers this kind of criticism in *The Curse of Cain: The Violent Legacy of Monotheism*. Schwarz argues that biblical monotheism is inescapably bound up with violence and that this tradition lies behind most, if not all, of Western civilization's evils. Because the Bible has formed and continues to form identity by designating a chosen people apart from others, Schwartz contends, it unavoidably provides divinely sanctioned justification for violence toward those outside the boundaries. "Violence," says Schwarz, "is not only what we do to the Other. It is prior to that. Violence is the very construction of the Other."[5]

Though critics like Schwarz do well to point out the often deadly behavior of monotheists, they seldom clarify exactly what the more peaceful alternatives are. Some argue that the world would be safer if people simply ignored the transcendent altogether, instead using more secular and practical ideologies to order the human community. Others suggest that Eastern religions such as Buddhism or Hinduism offer more peaceful alternatives to monotheism, and some turn to Native American religions as a surrogate.

However, religions outside of the three monotheisms have not done much better in checking violent impulses. Pre-Columbian Aztec and Incan cultures, for instance, often offered human sacrifices. At the dedication ceremony of the Aztec temple of Tenochtitlán, Mexico, in 1487, tribal leaders sacrificed as many as 84,400 captives.[6] So if monotheisms do have a record of violence, Peter

Berkowitz has noted, "it is equally true that plenty of cruelty and violence is on display in the pagan or non-biblically based religions of the world. . . . The Greek, the Norse and the Hindu gods are not exactly social democrats."[7]

In the United States, religions have justified slavery, the relocation or killing of Native Americans, and lynchings. But in twentieth-century America, there are almost certainly fewer deaths of citizens at the hands of others acting in the name of God than there are similar deaths around the world in any single week. This leads us to wonder, if religion is inherently violent, why has the United States, compared to other countries, been spared frequent and ongoing religious violence?

Providence, some would say, and did say back at the time of the country's founding. Founders who were cautious about their religious expression and wary about using biblical names for God often spoke of the blessings of Divine Providence. This provident God had given a spacious continent, rich in resources, with room enough for all, and had planted a set of peoples who, after reluctant and grudging moves, learned to accept each other.

Luck, say some. Luck in having all those resources. Luck in having founders who wrote a constitution that keeps the violent away from their victims and does not make it possible to legitimate a holy warrior's acting against other citizens. Luck that these founders adopted and advanced a philosophy born of the Enlightenment, a philosophy designed to promote generous views of other peoples and their faiths while allowing for and assuring freedom for each group to withhold consent from what others thought.

Learning, still others say. Most of the settlers from Europe knew what holy war had been like in and after the Reformation, the Thirty Years' War, the Puritan Revolutions, and a hundred uprisings—all in the name of God. They did not want to replicate it here.

In the end, most religious interpreters of American life congratulate their predecessors and contemporaries for "keeping cool" where group meets group, however hot the passion they bring to their faith.

Nonetheless, Americans dare not become complacent about religion's potential for violence. As the United States becomes more and more plural, many religious worldviews inevitably clash in discussions over the common good. Both worldwide and on the American scene, *fundamentalisms* display particular power. Though international versions have so far proved the most violent, their milder domestic counterparts shadow much of the controversy about American religion and politics. It is important, therefore, to recognize and understand fundamentalisms, as an awareness of them can deepen our public interactions while keeping us wary of religion's potential for dangerous action.

What Does Fundamentalism Look Like?

"All fundamentalists, whatever their pattern of relation to the world, seek purity, draw sharp ideological boundaries, value mission work, and want to avoid the evils of the fallen world even as they seek to redeem it."[8] Scholars agree that in spite of the differences among them, all fundamentalisms share some general features: adherence to fundamentals, dependence on modernity to trigger their response, reactivity, and "doing Jujitsu."

Adherence to Fundamentals

Protestant evangelicals embraced the term *fundamentalism* early in the twentieth century. They feared that "conservatives" were not firm enough and would not "do battle for the Lord." For them, fundamentalism was a badge of pride (although later some dropped the term because it also could be a stigma).

In examining fundamentalisms, we see that each of them, usually drawing on sacred writings and traditional teachings, identifies a cluster of beliefs that must be followed and defended. In the three monotheistic faiths, the fundamentals come from the Torah, the New Testament, and the Qur'an.

The Torah? Most scholars do not equate Jewish Orthodoxy or traditionalism with fundamentalism. The Orthodox and the traditional try to retain ancient ways of being Jewish, but most of them are not out to remake the world. Most are faithful to the covenant but do not hand out tracts and try to convert others at the airport. They may favor legislation that protects their sabbath, but they do not make efforts to use legislation to impose their will and practices on others. Yet there are some small movements, usually in the form of extremist support of Israel against the land claims of others, who lift out Torah passages and say that their stories show that God, in the promise to Moses, forever intended the land to be Israel's. Obviously, this fundamentalist view of the land cannot be a part of Muslim faith, and only a minority of Christians, fundamentalists themselves, agree in their own way with such claims about the land.

The New Testament? Again, Christians can be very traditional, for instance, in respect to liturgy and forms of worship; they can be orthodox in respect to the creeds and confessions of their communion; they can be "conservative," in that they try to hold to inherited patterns; they may agree with fundamentalists on the content of New Testament teaching; and yet they still wouldn't be considered fundamentalists. Christian fundamentalists insist on being militant and are standoffish with respect to other Christians, including evangelicals, regarded as dangerous by many fundamentalists. Fundamentalists are uncompromising and insist that biblical passages do not admit of more than one interpretation. Since Christian fundamentalism centers on witness to the biblical teachings about Jesus, these teachings or doctrines along with their separatism make Protestant fundamentalists distinctive. They share some forms but, with the exception of claims for Israel, none of the content of faith with Jews or Muslims.

The Qur'an? Non-Muslim Americans are busy learning that the Muslim fundamentalist with whom they became familiar in 1979 during the Iranian revolution is not the Muslim down the street. All orthodox Muslims believe that the Qur'an is the direct utterance of Allah through the prophet Muhammad, so scriptural "inerrancy" is not the mark of the Muslim fundamentalist. Wherever movements have arisen that many scholars call fundamentalist—

while noting that many Muslims use other terms—these have been movements that paid attention to literal applications of laws from Shari'a, a body of law.

Dependence on Modernity

Fundamentalist movements often seek the restoration of a golden age, a return to first principles, but scholars see fundamentalists as a distinctly modern combination of the old and the new. Though a politics of nostalgia leads fundamentalists to wish for a return to a world they believe they have lost, that world—while rooted in historical reality—is also a mythical construction. Scholars agree that fundamentalisms look very much like contemporary creations, fresh combinations of old spiritual raw materials with new goals and circumstances.

For example, some younger women in Muslim communities wear the *chador*, veiling their faces. Asked whether they do this because their mothers did, they might well say that they are doing it because their mothers did *not*. They have reached back beyond their parents' world and retrieved customs based on prescriptions that had been neglected or dismissed. Fearing that they will be overwhelmed by modernity and needing a badge of identity, they resurrect this symbol.

Similarly, Protestant fundamentalists are uncompromising in their biblical interpretation. For example, early in the twentieth century, their intellectual ancestors produced booklets called "The Fundamentals." Some of these expressed mild support for moderate versions of evolution. But when some of these fundamentalists deduced that more radical forms of evolution were being taught in public schools and their denominations' prestigious seminaries, they dug in and resisted all traces of evolutionary thinking in the sciences and in respect to scriptures. An aspect of modernity and modernization in theology triggered their fundamentalist response.

For all the similarities they bear to earlier movements, fundamentalists depend on modernity for their motivation—and their existence. Of course, modernity can mean many things. To some it would be best represented by technology. Not here. Almost all fundamentalist groups embrace the latest in technology and employ it toward "premodern" ends. Rather, if you let each group define it, modernity is whatever it is against which they know they must react. It can mean Westernization, as in much of the Arabic Muslim world. It can mean pluralism and relativism, which have eroded boundaries between true and false communities, true and false claims.

As Almond, Sivan, and Appleby put it, "While fundamentalists claim to be upholding orthodoxy (right belief) or orthopraxis (right behavior), and to be defending and conserving religious tradition and traditional ways of life from erosion, they do so by crafting new methods, formulating new ideologies, and adopting the latest processes and organizational structures."[9]

Reactivity

Both abroad and at home, fundamentalisms are reactive—*re + active*—movements. Fundamentalists find threatening certain features of contemporary life, and they react against those features by preserving their religious identities. Internationally, such threats include imperialism—hence the perception of the United States as the "Great Satan" by Iranian fundamentalists. In the United States, fundamentalists might feel threatened by a presumed conspiracy of "secular humanists" to keep religion carefully separated from public life. The Supreme Court gave credence to this belief in 1961 when it identified "Secular Humanism" as a religion. A year later, the Court disallowed prayer in public schools, and in 1963, teachers were barred from leading devotional readings of the Bible. While a Christian consensus seemed to reign over politics for most of America's first century, that consensus now appeared to be threatened by a Supreme Court grown hostile to the Judeo-Christian tradition. (The idea of reclaiming the culture for Christianity motivated more than fundamentalists. It propelled much of the New Christian Right into politics in the 1970s and 1980s.)

American fundamentalists perceive another threat in society's growing pluralism and its corollary, moral relativism—a term most fundamentalists did not use a few years ago. Instead, they talked about subversion by unbelieving theologians of their own communions, who supported progressive pursuits, evolution, or a variety of responses to moral change. Or they talked about everything as head-on satanic attacks on the bastion of truth.

Relativism strikes fundamentalists as the key feature of modernity, the main assault on the grasp of truth. Interestingly, relativism is a problem not because every system of thought, every contention, every moral decision is perceived as equally false. Just the opposite: they can all be presented positively by advocates, sold by the tolerant, until the victim of modernity decides that all truths are equally satisfying: You have yours. I have mine. I must tolerate you. What you believe makes no difference. I do not have to decide, or I can be eclectic, picking up bits and pieces from everywhere. And in the process, say not only fundamentalists, all seriousness in moral, intellectual, and spiritual searches gets sapped.

Doing Jujitsu

Jujitsu refers to the Japanese technique whereby seemingly weaker combatants can turn the strength of opponents to their advantage. Fundamentalists commonly perform a kind of Jujitsu on the forces that contemporary life throws against them. For example, modern mass media—including television, radio, and the Internet—tend to introduce a pluralism of ideas and options, something that might threaten the integrity of a fundamentalist worldview. While rejecting this effect, fundamentalists in America have turned the force of the mass media around, using it skillfully to bring their own message to the wider world.

On an intellectual level, fundamentalisms—especially American varieties—have performed Jujitsu on Enlightenment ideas. Liberal thinkers in the eighteenth and nineteenth centuries held to the supremacy of rational thought and often concluded that rationalism required the sloughing off of religious belief as mere superstition. Fundamentalists performed Jujitsu on this idea, claiming rationalism in service of faith. For example, when it seemed that scientific inquiry lent credence to an evolutionist view of human origins, many religious conservatives used the same kinds of scientific investigation and arguments to claim divine origins for human life.

One of the more ingenious reversals in American fundamentalism has to do with the way church and state are to relate. Most citizens believe that they should be somehow separate and distinguished, but there is no agreement on exactly what that means. Normally, they and their legal experts make an appeal to the First Amendment of the Constitution: "Congress shall make no law respecting an establishment of religion or prohibiting the free exercise thereof." Many go on to say that the intention was to have a godless Constitution (unlike most constitutions elsewhere), thus allowing citizens freedom to develop their moral and theological commitments without state imposition or guidance. And others went still further to say that the founders tended not to be orthodox Christians but Deists or Enlightenment religionists who were respectful of Christianity but thought you could have a moral and virtuous republic on general philosophical grounds, being subject to natural law, natural reason, and reason's god.

Then along comes modern fundamentalism or political evangelicalism. It takes the force of modernity's assault and argues that *if* the founders had a somewhat independent faith, then that faith, called "secular humanism," is illegally privileged and established. And if the founders were more orthodox—and fundamentalists regard all but one or two, such as Thomas Jefferson, as "Bible believers"—then one must look at what their original intention had to be. In this argument, they claim that the First Amendment still allowed governmental support for religion to continue, if all religions benefit legally. Most consistently, they argue that the establishment clause tells what only *Congress* cannot do—leaving the states free to do their own improvising.

The Potential for Religious Violence:
Liberal and Secular Alternatives

Reactive religious movements are hardly the only ones with the potential to disrupt the civil order. For all its devotion to tolerance, moderate or liberal religion has often taken intolerant forms.

We have made it clear that fundamentalist disruption of the American civil order almost never takes the form of violence or life-taking that it takes in much of the rest of the world. Instead it tends to take forms that are verbal or gestured—through images in cartoons, disdainful and demeaning remarks, and incivility, all of which make the constructive addressing of social issues more difficult.

So it is with liberal complication and disruption. If you do not believe so, ask your friendly neighborhood fundamentalist or intense member of the Christian Right. The rightist complains that all the attention falls on the rightist camp because the media are biased by liberal outlooks or because liberals are suave and subversive about the way they hold exclusionary power.

Liberal disruption shows up in primary and secondary schools, especially in the areas of sex education and social commentary. There liberals tend to acquiesce in the idea that they cannot prevent all teenagers from having sex, so they promote health causes, such as the counsel to use condoms. They might want to advance the notion that homosexual lifestyles are acceptable. They teach not a well-defined set of moral truths but "values clarification." All these are abhorrent signs of liberal incivility to their opponents. These foes see liberals as having sneaked or forced their way into positions from which they can propagate their ideas and subvert systems. In place of condoms, the religious literalists say, why not simply promote abstinence as the only foolproof method for preventing teenage pregnancy? Why not quote the Bible's several passages against homosexual behavior and be done with it? Why assume that all the value systems children bring need clarifying before the student engages in moral action? The Bible has clarified values once and for all; who are the liberals to have forced their way into the world of textbooks, libraries, teacher training programs, school boards, and the like?

Liberals, their critics will tell them, "used" religion in support of the civil rights movement and various post–New Deal, post–New Frontier, post–Great Society causes. In all of these they invoked God—who was working through Martin Luther King Jr. or the National Conference of Catholic Bishops or the National Council of Churches or denominational headquarters. Who asked them to do that? How did they get into the position of helping those causes, and who gave them the monopoly on interpreting them as God's doing?

Liberals were most prominent in opposing the Vietnam War, which they had helped develop. Liberal "brightest and best" scholars and agents had prompted the escalation of the war in 1965, but they did not want to be reminded of that as they scourged Bible-quoting "hawks." When fundamentalists gravitated to the hawkish position, liberals dismissed them as less than godly, God being the God of pacifists.

Talk about intolerance, say their critics; just look at the liberal religionists. They tend to speak about dialogue and conversation but are unwilling to listen on the subject of abortion. They may not be as open about using theology to justify their commitment to "choice" as their opponents will be with justifying "life," but the theology is there. And they disrupt church and civil life by supporting gay rights far beyond constitutional demands. Their expanded definitions of the family have undercut the traditional family. They are so sure they must support freedom of speech that they limit "our" freedom of religion, which finds so much speech to be blasphemous, obscene, immoral—and needing limits in law. They are not tolerant or dialogical about these matters, and in their own way, they call God down on their side. Religion, in its varied forms, seems to promote violence.

Would Nonreligion Avoid Violence?

Clearly, religion can cause trouble, even of the most deadly kind. The frequency and near universality of religiously motivated violence can make any reasonable person wonder if religion and politics might best be kept completely separate. Better to cordon off religion from politics before passions get out of hand.

Yet many twentieth-century attempts to replace religion with nonreligion have only issued in more violence. The century's totalitarians, intending to be non- and antireligious, opposed the historic faiths. Yet the concentration camps and gulags, the famines induced by bad policies, the destruction of sacred art in cultural revolutions, the murder of priests behind barbed wire, and genocidal policies were effected not in the name of Allah or Yahweh or the Father of Jesus Christ or any of the gods. Who can speak credibly in the name of the natural humaneness of nonreligion?

If religions have a spotty historical record when it comes to violence and nonreligious alternatives have fared no better, what's left? A world of benevolent anarchy perhaps? People inevitably organize themselves into groups, tribes, or nations, so to advocate a nonorganized alternative is unrealistic. People will gather together on the basis of various identities, including religious ones. So the question remains: Do religions have a proper place in the political sphere, or will they cause more trouble than other means of organization?

Political Interaction Compromises Religion's Purity

Some observers have insisted that the purity of both church and state is best served by keeping them apart. Virginia Baptist John Leland, arguing against general state support for religion, wrote that "government has no more to do with the religious opinions of men than it has with the principles of mathematics."[10] Other Baptists have also played a prominent role in a long line of religious Americans seeking to keep church and state separate. Isaac Backus, whom we have already met as a prime New England Baptist, was a dissenter against the establishment's mingling of church and state. And Baptists like to claim as one of their own Roger Williams, the Massachusetts and Rhode Island pioneer, in keeping the government out of religion and religion out of government.

In our own time, Baptists of the North and South, who could not agree on many things, produced a "joint commission" to draw a clear line between church and state. They were often friends of the courts when that line needed redefinition. During the mid-twentieth century, many helped form a group (often anti-Catholic in its impulses) called Protestants and Other Americans United for Separation of Church and State.

For decades it was a badge of pride in the Southern Baptist Convention that it "stayed out of politics," except for considerable opposition to the presidential campaign of Catholic Al Smith in 1928 and repeal of Prohibition through the 1920s. That stance has changed in our own time, when recent Southern Baptist Convention votes have supported prayer in the public schools and similar policies that, in the eyes of their critics, blur or cross the line between church and state.

In contemporary America, many religious people stand in the tradition of Backus and Leland. Some feel that the purity of religion would be compromised by the inevitable give-and-take of political activity. Others, across the religious spectrum, fear that the words of religious leaders will unfairly cause a political reaction against all adherents of that particular faith, working against denominational and congregational purposes. As but one example, as recently as the spring of 1999, Cal Thomas and Ed Dobson, prominent members of the Christian Right, questioned the direct political tactics of the right for its overidentification with the Republican party and joined others in questioning whether the tactics might not be hurting both the political and the religious causes. It was time to change the culture, out of which better politics would come, they argued. In order for faith to remain pure and prosper, they went on, a proper distance between church and state must be maintained.

Religion and Politics: Is the Mix Worth the Risk?

This brief catalogue of the dangers—both real and potential—of intermingling religion and politics points toward an obvious conclusion: America will be better off if religion and politics are kept far apart. At best, religion causes division in the political realm. At worst, religion causes all kinds of deadly trouble. Perhaps religiously motivated political action has no place in a democratic republic.

The next chapter offers a substantial rejoinder to this argument. Although religion and politics can often be a combustible mix, there are many reasons for assuming that religion will continue to be involved in politics and for advocating that it be so.

2

Worth the Risk

Public Religion and the Common Good

*Thesis: Public religion can and does contribute to the
common good.*

Scene 1: Like millions of other Americans, you toss a dollar or
ten into the red bucket of the Salvation Army bell-ringer in De-
cember. You all must feel that the Army does good work. Otherwise,
you would not respond to the appeal for contributions. No similar
charity has a broader appeal or raises more funds.

The word *salvation* suggests to you that something religious
prompts the "Salvationists" to weather the sleet and buck the winds
of urban corners. Unless you are one of the fewer than half a million Americans who are part of the "inclusive membership" of this
disciplined organization, you may not know personally a single
member of the Salvation Army. You may even be a bit uneasy about
the military terminology that serves to describe the group. It is also
highly unlikely that you would have sat down with a Salvationist
to discuss the fine points of the "Articles of War" that all must sign,
and you would be lost making your way through the eleven articles
of the Wesleyan Arminian Holiness teachings that make this evangelical group distinctive.

So distinctive is the group that when it was first organized, other
Christians were alarmed by many of its practices. Salvationists do
not baptize or celebrate the Lord's Supper. Their private teachings

and worship offended even that most tolerant observer of religious enthusiasm, philosopher William James. In 1897, in *The Will to Believe*, James busied himself "defending the legitimacy of religious faith" against some rationalist critics who regarded such an effort as "a sad misuse of one's professional position." He had to admit that he ran out of patience with some groups and as far as the Salvation Army was concerned, "what such audiences most need is that their faiths should be broken up and ventilated, that the northwest wind of science should get into them and blow their sickliness and barbarism away."

All those irritants to other Christians, rationalists, and observers such as James belonged to what we might call the private side of the Salvation Army. During the century since James wrote, the Army and the culture have changed. Today it is the public face of the Army that moves people. Let the Salvationists do what they wish to spread salvation; we are impressed that they serve human needs. Is the Army involved with the public? Indeed. The majority of the dollars it puts to work come from public revenues, from tax subsidies. Told that this is the case, most people shrug and don't even bring up whether this practice violates the separation of church and state. They have positively assessed the public good served by this private group.

Scene 2: Although your uncles and aunts may have resisted the civil rights movement, dragged their feet when asked to march for justice in the 1960s, or felt that the Reverend Martin Luther King Jr. had lost his charm before you ever found it, in their old age they are likely to take a different view of the movement, the marches, the Baptist pastor, and his coleaders. You may have resisted a King national holiday, and you may hang out with people who still enjoy regaling each other with stories about his private life that were gathered by the FBI. Yet it is hard to argue with the point that overall the legacy of the movement and the man is a positive good. Even social conservatives and people who believe you cannot legislate morality recognize gains in realizing justice among the races. The cleric whose face could have been on "Wanted" posters in many a community before 1968 is now pictured in classrooms and buildings as an American hero.

Of course, millions of Americans are unwaveringly positive about this Nobel Prize winner and champion of nonviolence, who may indeed have prevented bloodbaths. Among these supporters may be agnostics or atheists. Many are undoubtedly Jews, who massively supported the civil rights cause, even though King's organization bore the name Southern *Christian* Leadership Conference. Most of these people were moved by the preacher's rhetoric, not by the substance of his gospel. Many may not have realized that he treated the U.S. Constitution and the Declaration of Independence as sacred documents, texts for his public religion. But they could not have missed the fact that he took the faith expressed in texts from the prophets and the gospels, nurtured in private homes and small churches, and put it to work to effect change in law and attitude. This was public religion in action.

Scene 3: It would be false to the nature of religion to measure it only by its charities and its occasional contribution to the workings of justice. Faith also has to do with interpreting life and contributing to the search for meaning. Through religion, citizens find meaning that goes beyond doing good and being good. Of course, religion as interpretation is double-sided in its effects. People oppress and hate and kill in its name and under its thrall. Yet at least on many occasions, as in the slave quarters, among the abolitionists, on the tongues of peacemakers and reconcilers such as Abraham Lincoln in his Second Inaugural Address, and when clergy help communities deal with tragedy and move on toward reconstruction, "public religion" appears to the vast majority as a positive good. And as an element in the interpreting of life, fulfilling religion also and always impels the prophetic note to be bounced back into the lives of people. They are supposed to be self-critical or to respond to divine criticism and judgment, to be reformed, and to renew the republic.

It is one thing to point to the presence of religion and begin to describe or define some of its manifestations. It is another to suggest, as we did in the previous chapter, that the introduction and exploitation of religion in politics and government can be a distraction or a menace. And it is yet another to adduce reasons why religion can be a good in the public order.

Yale law professor Stephen Carter has complained about the "trivialization" of religion in respect to politics and law in America. The present exercise falls into the family of what, reversing Carter, we might call the "detrivialization" of religion in politics and government.

What good has religion done, and what good can it do? Consider the following eighteen reasons, a starter set for a list that could be extended. Some items will strike readers as idealizations of religion, while others will describe characteristics that only some religious people share. Think of these less as irrefutable facts and more as directional pointers and conversation starters.

Religion Is Not Going to Disappear

Religion will not go away. Among those for whom religion is important, it is supremely important. Of course, merely pointing to the pervasiveness of religion is not enough. After all, cancer also exists, and so do noxious weeds, and our energies are usually spent working against them. Why should we work for, and not against, religion in the public arena?

Religion Deals with the Deepest Elements of Life

To those who demonstrate active and assertive attitudes toward faith, be it formal or informal, communal or individual, left or right in its propulsion of energies, there is no way to conceive of morality, ethics, and action on profound causes without recourse to those deepest religious fonts of thought, belief, and action. It is unnatural, unrealistic, and unsatisfying to ask a public servant to park his or her faith at the door when helping decide whether the nation will go to war or wage peace, whether government should be an agent in attending to welfare of the dispossessed, or whether people should pursue mere self-interest or mix that interest with the common good. To be sure, thoughtful leaders with profound religious convictions will be sensitive to the demands and expectations of a pluralistic society. Such leaders likely cannot be effective public servants if they press particularistic claims in general society. But when making their decisions with the good of the broader public in mind, they are also likely to take those precise particularities into consideration.

So it is with constituencies, participants in electoral processes, and the governed in general: to expect them to form coalitions and caucuses motivated by everything other than religion—concerns of gender, race, ethnicity, class, aesthetics, interest, ideology—is unrealistic and "against the rules" in a constitutional republic. But as with the governors, so with the governed: they take calculated risks if they demand that they have their way on the basis of the particularities of their faith. Such action might well inspire backlash, counterorganization by others, or expressions of distaste for their faith. Yet they can see the positive good in religious movements that, for all their differences, can be allied for the common good.

Religion Is Already at Work in the Public Arena

A republic would be better off if everyone brought into the open whatever motivates and impels the citizens to decide and to act. Through the centuries and recent decades, different claimants have taken the initiative in putting religion to work in the public sphere. Support for the welfare state and civil rights and opposition to some wars came from congregations, denominations, and ecumenical forums. Support for organized labor often received a great impetus from Catholics and other churches. Support for Israel and for liberal rights and social causes came from Jews. Urban political measures drew overt support from African American congregations. The peace churches lobbied for peace. One cannot write the history of positive human achievement without reckoning with such contributions, and one must acknowledge that a republic is most healthy when all views, including religious views, are present in public debate.

Religion Provides Public Conversation with Needed Resources

Another reason for bringing religion into the open has to do with the resources it brings. We have heard modern thinkers rely on ancient religious texts to explain things "because they already knew back then what we do not know as yet." These texts include important themes of prophecy and criticism that will not get voiced by other than religious people. It is not likely that a Martin Luther King Jr. could have achieved much of what he did had he not been dealing with a populace that felt it should make some response to what he reminded them Isaiah and Jesus and Paul said. Environmentalists often draw on unconventional and minority faiths, many of them from the East, to line up votes and promote care for the environment, and they do so more successfully than those who argue merely prudentially.

Religion Helps Illuminate the Presuppositions of All Conversation Partners

Bringing faith into the open in politics and government is also one means of "smoking out" other latent ideologies in the republic. Sometimes in an academic or civil forum, people will root their arguments in Marxist, Adam Smithian, feminist, gay, middle-class, and other ideologies disguised as self-evident ways of life. Just as with thieves spotting thieves, so with religionists in law observance: it takes one to know one. Religious people can point to elements in the worldview or propaganda of the other, the nonreligious element, that may have undisclosed and unrecognized metaphysical backgrounds and interests.

Religion Can Bring Perspective and Help Diminish Political Fanaticisms

Religion in the public order can serve to relativize other elements in that order and help bring contested items into perspective. Religionists may not always do well with their perspectives, but they are called to be responsive to the eternal and also to possess a longer view of the shorter-term temporal order. Faith can point to the limits of politics and reveal it as an aspect of life that can easily aspire to become the unlimited, the infinite, the all-consuming. A book title suggests a valid reminder from the religious world: *Everything Is Politics, but Politics Is Not Everything.*[1] When the religious remember that and live by it, they can help quicken electorates from apathy without summoning them to political zealotry. Faith can help citizens learn to take something very, very seriously—but not too seriously. While ordinary people can point to the genuine hopes that come with political investment, they can also lose heart when their causes do not prosper, or they can become prideful when they succeed. The voice of faith in the political context calls for other, different responses.

Religious Freedom Helps Assure All Other Freedoms

Religion in governmental life is still "the first freedom." The First Amendment places it there. James Madison and other founders made much of the proposition. Where religion prospers anywhere in the world, other freedoms follow or are attached to it. So it is that devotion to religion and religious freedoms helps the cause of liberty across the board. Many of the fanatics for religious freedom may approach it in a skewed manner and may not care as much for the common good of the republic as for their own souls or communities. That makes little difference for this issue—though it has more importance in others—since these restless seekers of their own liberty force rethinking on everyone else. Over the long run, the larger population has seen the value of making room for extremists of faith.

Religion Can Combat Apathy

Putting religion to work can be a means of quickening more voters to rise out of apathy. For example, people in a community may not notice the need for new nursing home legislation until their home church calls them to service regarding a badly run facility. Very often it has been and remains the religious agency and community that has welcomed the immigrant and engaged in relief. The religious call is constant, insistent, "for all seasons," and can outlast appeals of merely moralistic character.

Religious Communities Are Practiced and Durable

Religious communities often keep classes, conversations, and caucuses going in a time of general public apathy. In congregations and other religious groups, people encounter those who are only in some ways like-minded. Many members do burrow down into more specialized camps to gather strength for participating in political wars, but others take advantage of belonging to groups that may bring together various interests and meet on the basis of relative consensus.

Religions Can Contribute to Conversations About the Common Good

Most religions have what we might call "theologies of public order," thoughts about the common good that provide interpretations of the workings of the body politic and the forces in it. However, they do not express these interpretations if their adherents exclude themselves, or feel themselves excluded, from contention in the public arena. Why might it be good to have these theologies evident in public life? The record of the twentieth century has shown that when one ideology, one leadership group, or any majority seeks a monopoly, a variety of voices can help assure freedom.

Religious People Can Draw on Overlooked Resources

In the United States, "secular rationality" has a central place in political thinking, but religious groups accent other themes that also have their place. Among these we might list community, tradition, memory, intuition, affection, and hope. There is a double-sidedness to all of these, of course. Community can be exclusive. Tradition often weighs people down and limits their imagination. One cannot live in the past, which is where memory turning to nostalgia imprisons people. Intuition can go wrong. Affection extended to one's own may rule out "the other." Hope can easily turn into optimism and thus toward foolishness. But the positive contributions of each of these are great assets in a republic. Though it is not possible to base a pluralist republic on any one of these, each helps ensure that more interests, more people, and more dimensions of life get their hearing.

Religious People Can Provide a Voice for the Voiceless

Voices of religion can be heard where other voices are silent or where "secular rationality" is not effective. The fetus, the comatose, the mentally limited, the defenseless—all these need representation not only by secular rationalists but also by those who value what cannot always be reduced to logic, to the bartering of power based on calculated self-interest, and the like.

Religions Are Distinctively Qualified to Revitalize the Republic

Religious voices can help the larger society recover, appraise, and criticize some neglected themes that can benefit political and governmental life. It is easy, for example, to forget the power of stewardship, which is a strong element in most religions but not something on which self-interested people will reflexively draw. In times when ambition and careerism are given such a high value, the concept of vocation, as in "a vocation to public service," can help ennoble the lives of people in politics. A third religious idea that is often neglected by self-seekers in governmental life is mission. Recovery of a sense of mission can help guide people in political entities in times of drift.

Religiously Motivated Citizens Are Committed for the Long Term

Religious faith at its best involves people with outlooks on government that will sustain them in hard times. If one is truly committed to a faith, consequences follow. The religious can "hang in there," no matter what the present circumstances. They do not merely follow the trends of the moment or lose heart when the going is tough. Any number of causes in American public life—one thinks of abolition, civil rights, the rights of laborers, the protection of children—have attracted their cohorts of fickle "Sunday soldiers." However, people of faith, through prophecy and criticism, gesture and witness, often find reason to stay with their commitments.

Religions Often Encourage Dealing Positively with the Other

Religions can breed fanaticism and thus can disrupt political discourse among those who hold to such beliefs. But a commitment this side of fanaticism, which marks most religions, can lead faith-filled participants in political life to find new motives for dealing with "the other."

Religions Provide Stamina for Dealing with Crises

At their best, faiths instill noble ideals and help people form habits and follow customs on which to draw in crisis. These may not be patent in the day-to-day of political and governmental life. But at times, as when President Abraham Lincoln called on them as "the better angels of our nature," they can serve as a potential. Not that they always do appear, nor are religious people always attentive to them. But developing these better aspects of personal life and culture is part of the claims and aspirations of people of faith.

Religions Offer Chances for Renewal

In the repertory of options that most faiths seek to stock are repentance and the call to be purified, to turn. Again, nonbelievers can also find new resolve and make fresh resolutions. But in political and governmental life, where the stakes are high and mistakes are expensive, the ability to humble oneself in the face of God, of the sacred, to find motives for drastic change and consequent self-improvement, is important too. It can affect a cause, a party, and a nation.

Religions Can Help Protect the Individual in the World of Politics

Most faiths, and not least of all the prophetic religions of Judaism and Christianity, have great regard for what political philosopher Glenn Tinder calls "the exalted individual."[2] Believers conceive of each person as having been created "in the image of God." A Christian gloss on this is the Incarnation, in which God honors the human

race by joining it in the person of Jesus Christ. Honoring the exalted individual and stressing the dignity of the human are major
preoccupations of other religions as well. Whatever else religions
do in political life, they hold the individual in high regard. They
will not always do well at this, and they will not be the only ones
who do so, but they have special motivations for staying with this
preoccupation.

Amending the List

You will certainly be able to add many more points to this adver-
tisement for the positive potential of some religious expression in
some situations in some views of the public order. Of course, you
will also want to call into question some of the rather bold claims
we have just set forth. After all, there will always be days when we
have to cross our fingers or hold our noses when observing what can
happen in the name of religion gone public.

"Public religion" is not a top-down, worked-out, authoritative
concept. It is the result of the very complex strivings and question-
ings of a couple of hundred million citizens. How it is realized in
contemporary life depends on the quality of the questioning, the
clarity of people's expression, and the seriousness of their resolve as
individual citizens.

3

The Individual Citizen, Formed and Mobilized by Faith

Thesis: Individual citizens are energized by an awareness of possibilities based on their beliefs, and the effects of those beliefs provide hope for improving the republic.

When two gun-toting teenagers killed numbers of their schoolmates at Columbine High School in Littleton, Colorado, in 1999, the citizenry screamed to legislators: "Do something!" Soon there were moves to address one of the issues, the easy availability of firearms. No one believed that stricter gun control measures would prevent incidents like that at Columbine, but many thought that such measures could be part of an arsenal of instruments ensuring restraint. Congress, state legislatures, and city councils scrambled to meet some of the new demands. Polls showed the public overwhelmingly on the side of these demands. Yet were the public's representatives listening to the public? Perhaps, but they were listening harder to particular lobbies and interest groups. These groups were acting perfectly legally, but their pressure trumped the power of the electorate.

Some voters interpret the Second Amendment to the United States Constitution in such a way that they believe "religiously" that gun ownership is their right, a sacred right, and that any restrictions violate it. Others interpret the Constitution in a different

way and see no conflict between regulations on gun sales, ownership, and use and the two-century-old intention that citizens be prepared when called to form militias. For many of these people, "Thou
shalt not kill" is a divine and inviolate command, and those who
make it easy for young people and dangerous elements in society to
arm themselves are participants in killing. Are their voices and arguments heard when the time to vote has come?

Sometimes long-brewing political issues boil over so suddenly
that few people have a chance to debate them. In such instances,
only strong special-interest groups may have opportunity to reach
legislators. It is too late for citizens to elect representatives who reflect their views, including their religious ones, on the matter. Representatives are already in place. They are forced to vote. A
deadline is near. The lobbyists are at their door—or have made their
way inside already—and they will be heard. All that ordinary citizens can do is wait for the next election and try to advance someone who is more congenial to their personal outlook.

The day of an election or of a vote on legislation is a crucial moment in lawmaking, whether the public attaches moral or religious
connotations to the outcome or not. But what gets overlooked is
that most such choices of candidates and of legislative positions
have long histories. The choices get debated in town meetings, city
councils, church basements, service clubs, denominational and congregational assemblies, and family circles. In these settings, citizens
with a longer view have the chance to have their religious opinions
heard.

Take the issue of capital punishment. The matter is much debated;
both sides have had two centuries—some would say two millennia—
to find heroes, principles, and texts. Yet even so, not all options are
neatly foreclosed in respect to the issue. On occasion a born-again
person on death row is so convincing in testifying to his or her conversion and changed life that ordinarily vehement supporters of the
death penalty have second thoughts. Or law students will pursue
the cases of people on death row and find numbers of them falsely

charged and unjustly committed. This causes growing agitation to reexplore the meaning and effectiveness, the motives for and out-comes of death penalty laws. Yet the time to shape opinion is less on the night of an execution, when only a Supreme Court order or a governor's conscience can intervene, than in the long days and years when pro and con religious voices can bring insights from their traditions.

Or consider this: a state has a huge budget surplus. What should the legislature do with it? One set of people believes religiously that the excess of tax-generated funds is theirs. They earned the money. They paid the taxes. They should get back what they earned if it's not needed. The Bible says so, and fairness demands it. Another set of people believes religiously that poor people have been treated un-justly by the taxing authorities. They have paid in disproportion-ately to the state treasury. Now, in surplus times, is the chance to do justice and love mercy and return funds to them or, more likely, to social causes that will benefit them—usually, for example, by pro-viding better education. Such believers will support what they call a just distribution, but often to little effect.

Picture a situation, however, in which the people in the churches, the causes, and the interest groups have for years been teaching themselves and others that there are alternative ways to assess taxes more fairly and to redistribute tax funds more equitably when opportunities arise. They have had their own minds made up. They have presented the case and converted others, in living rooms, parish halls, wherever. They have taught them the ways that they think justice lines up with what Isaiah said or the Muslim commu-nity has long thought. Here is another instance where religion in politics has effective means short of, this side of, before, and in a way despite what goes on in the voting booth or on the legislature's floor.

Consider yet another public dilemma: the increasing ways to keep someone alive in a vegetative state. Through the years, ad-vancing technology has created ever more complex circumstances, and legislators have to come up with instruments for helping society cope with such change. Can physician-assisted suicide be permitted? Must health maintenance organizations and other agencies pay for all care as long as there is a pulse, even in a brain-dead person? Can those who believe that humans should not "play God" by intervening in the dying process have their conscientious viewpoints heard? Can they make it heard on more than the day of a legislative vote or an election of representatives who see this as only one of hundreds of issues in any session?

Here again, citizens in politics have earlier and more ample roles to play. They can show up in discussions of practices in particular hospitals. They are heard when families gather to debate "pulling the plug" on an aged relative. They speak from pulpits and through interest groups. They have a hearing when medical ethicists, especially those informed by theological ethics, do their debating.

Citizen involvement thus occurs on many levels and behind many scenes, and the religious representation is both most needed and most effective *before* candidates and specific pieces of legislation come into the picture.

We live in political societies, and both people who vote and those who do not have an influence, be it informed and judicious or not. And let us not forget the individual who gets elected or appointed to public office or who heads an interest group. His or her conscience is of great importance here. To whom does this person listen? What texts motivate this person? How ready is this person to go against what is popular because of conviction that this or that policy is God-pleasing, most congruent with natural law, or expressive of the moral self—as opposed to what is merely expedient?

There is a bottom line to all this: in a political society such as ours and in a free republic, while there are limits to politics, politics relates to ways of life that involve the knowledge, responsibility, conscience, connections, and commitments of ordinary citizens, citizens as believers. So let us look at the role of the individual.

Individual Citizens and Public Religion

"I bid you to a one-man revolution— / The only revolution that is coming," wrote Robert Frost.[1] Any discussion of public religion and politics rightfully begins with the individual. Though Frost's second line is debatable, his first-line invitation rings true: considerable change begins with individual decisions. All talk about what agencies and institutions might do is idle if individuals do not initiate change. And for all the strength of communal life, belonging to a religious community does not commit everyone to think or vote the same way. Fellow believers may band together on certain issues— Mormons may generally agree on free enterprise, and most Methodists may oppose gambling—but they are not ordinarily impelled to do so. If religion is to contribute to politics, then, we dare not wait for faith-based communities to reach unanimity on issues. Individual, religiously motivated citizens can and must contribute as individuals to the political process.

There are many ways in which this individual activity has its effect.

Rosa Parks engaged in political action when she refused to move to the back of the bus in Montgomery in 1955, early in the civil rights movement. She was a devout churchgoer, but how much her church membership and faith contributed to her moral fabric and stamina it may be hard to tell, and she may have had the most difficulty of anyone to sort out the mix of motives and intentions. But she demonstrated what one ordinary citizen can do. In consequence, along come movements that bring expertise and the ability to endure and enlarge on her action.

Sometimes politics begins with nothing more than a gesture or witness by an individual. For instance, a particular young man in conscience could not permit himself to respond when drafted during the late stages of the Vietnam War. The public through its legislators has long made room for religious dissent and expression by conscientious objectors against all wars. But this person was not a pure pacifist and could not swear—we have said he was a person who acted "in conscience" and thus was "of conscience"—that he would *never* respond to the call of arms in any war. But by no "just war" criteria could he participate in this one. He was willing to take alternative service, but the law did not provide for "selective conscientious objection." He was a Lutheran, who read Luther for guidance. He convinced himself that Luther, no dove about things military, said that if your "lord"—we are talking feudalism—calls you to fight in a cause you know to be unjust and you kill, that is murder.

He asked for backing from the congregation to which he belonged. The parishioners admired him for all that he had done for the youth of the church, for his representing their ministry in the urban ghetto near them, for his overseas service. The leadership called for an open hearing that anyone could attend. What would they think if he fled to Sweden or Canada? Some members, in conscience, were vehement. They had shouldered a gun against Nazism; why could he not do so against communism? If the congregation listened to his thinking and the impulse spread, who would ever come to the defense of the country? Countryhood and its defense did not strike these church members as antibiblical. Another set spoke in favor of supporting whatever he would do to avoid the draft, so that he would have a sense of their backing even where they could not find legal means to support him.

The man ended up going to Canada and, several years later, found their backing for his return. We tell the story not to settle the issue of selective conscientious objection, a cause to which no one pays attention when there is no war or draft and to which few respond when there is. Its place here is to show that people of differing convictions can have theological warrants for what they do. They can learn from hearing each other, even when the speaking gets heated. And over the long haul, the action of an individual citizen, though it might not issue in clear legislation or "solve" any-thing, can contribute to the moral fabric of the political order.

In instances too numerous and mundane to mention, an indi-vidual will appear at a town board and witness, with effect. Suppose that a cluster of congregations want to provide for the homeless in their area. Suppose—and one need not do much supposing because the instances have been so frequent—that some property owners oppose any kind of sheltering of these homeless by churches in their community. Suppose that the churches are ready to back off because they want and need the goodwill of their community, beginning with the town board. The hearings come to a decisive stage, and the antis have been well heard. Then one citizen stands up and, to the astonishment of all, tells the story of his own days as a home-less person, taken in by a church group when he was down and out and given a chance to become the responsible citizen they now know. The town board summons the courage to change the direc-tion of its vote—all because of one individual.

Or an individual may motivate other individuals to witness to effect. Take the case of a minister who called for months on an aged woman, abandoned by her family, in a home for the aged. From the beginning, he was suspicious of the place because of the impersonal and even rude staff and because of the casual nature of the care. As she neared death, she requested that he provide a church service and some sort of token congregation to note and mourn her pass-ing. This he did. He wrote a note to attach to the home's records and the patient's file: If she dies between my calls, summon me at once. Three weeks later he called, only to find that she had died two weeks before. His efficient and careful signals had gone unheeded by a heedless staff. He was disappointed. No, enraged. Soon he found that this home, like others in the community, gave inadequate care because of very lax state regulations for monitoring and holding homes to standards. Our ordinary "individual citizen" minister was soon stirring his congregation and others in the area. Before long, several buses were bound to the state capitol for the next round of social legislation in respect to nursing homes. The legislature heard from a previously unstirred group—and acted, thus using political means to help ensure better care.

Individual Citizens as Officeholders

Individual citizens may also be officeholders whose conscience calls them to particular gestures even when the votes are not present, to particular witness even when they know they will alienate interests that will back their opponents in the next election. Is there a role for personal religious conviction in the officeholder's execution of duty? What if this conflicts with the convictions of those whom the officeholder represents or on whose behalf he or she acts?

Executives

In his Farewell Address in 1796, George Washington proclaimed: "Of all the dispositions and habits, which lead to political prosperity, Religion and morality are indispensable supports. In vain would that man claim the tribute of Patriotism, who should labour to subvert these great Pillars of human happiness, these firmest props of the duties of Men and Citizens. . . . Let us with caution indulge the supposition, that morality can be maintained without religion. . . . Reason and experience both forbid us to expect, that national morality can prevail in exclusion of a religious principle."

Wanting Our Leaders to Be Religious

Picture a European participant in the conversation about the interaction of religion and politics in the United States. Her social scientific texts have prepared her to understand America as a secular nation: church and state are kept separate. Then why, she will ask, do American citizens want their leaders to be religious? If the United States is secular, tolerant, and pluralist, why do citizens encourage and cherish public professions of faith by their leaders? Why do they expect their leaders, especially the president, to exemplify morality, knowing that morality is inevitably connected with religion? Especially in the eyes of outsiders, American attitudes must seem at best inexplicable, at worst hypocritical.

The desire for individualized religion to shape individual leaders stands in a long American tradition that goes all the way back to the nation's founders. Until having "killed the king" by declaring independence from Great Britain, most colonists had believed that God had endowed the king to rule by divine right. With the king off the scene and with government in the hands of freely chosen legislative, executive, and judicial leaders under a written constitution, the question arose, How could the continuing presence of morality be assured?

Democracy depended on a virtuous citizenry who would voluntarily follow a moral course. Since sovereignty now resided in the people, virtue would be reinforced only through spiritual and intellectual associations of the citizenry's creation. Righteous citizens could be shaped by the teachings and practices of any number of religions. It made little difference which religion was involved; being religious in general was all that mattered.

In the 1960 presidential campaign, when Richard Nixon, running against Catholic John Kennedy, was given the chance to exploit anti-Catholic feelings, he demurred, saying, "I, personally, would never raise the question and would not tolerate any use of the religious issue by anyone connected with my campaign. . . . There were several questions as to Kennedy's qualifications for the presidency, but I never at any time considered his religion in this category."[2] Religion, said Nixon, would be an issue only if a candidate "had no religious belief." (What that said about fairness to agnostics and atheists, who have equal constitutional rights, is itself revealing about the American populace and its sentiments.)

It was important, he said, that a candidate have a "basic belief in God," but beyond that religion should not matter. Nixon was no doubt correct in assuming that the public wanted religion to be a part of a candidate's commitments. He was safe in stating this while knowing that no one would ask such further questions as "Which religions would be acceptable?" or "What aspects of each would further the public good?"

Expectations of Presidential Religiosity

"There were very few occasions," former president Jimmy Carter recalled, "when I felt torn between my own faith and my obligation to comply with my oath to 'preserve, protect, and defend the Constitution of the United States.' There is probably not a great incompatibility between our patriotic ideals for America and Judeo-Christian values. Justice, equal opportunity, human rights, freedom, democracy, truth—those are the kinds of things that were spelled out by Thomas Jefferson and others in the founding days of our country, and we still would like to preserve them."[3]

The voters who elected Jimmy Carter, Ronald Reagan, George Bush, and Bill Clinton to the highest office of the land found plenty of piety and social commitment behind these presidents' campaigns and administrations. These presidents cultivated religious leaders and were in turn judged by those religious leaders who disagreed with them politically, theologically, and—in the case of Clinton especially—morally. But while all seemed to meet the public's requirement of being generally religious, each had difficulty translating his religion into public policy when it came to specific issues.

As a Baptist, Jimmy Carter spoke often of "soul liberty" and declared that he had to pay great attention to human rights in international affairs. He did, and at times this made foreign policy more difficult to execute. Ronald Reagan self-consciously identified with the domestic programs of the religious right, just as he welcomed their support for increased military expenditures to wage the Cold War against the "evil empire" of the Soviets. But he ran afoul of other religious leaders when his Central American foreign policy violated the moral sensibilities of many Catholics and Protestants. In 1991, most Episcopal leaders opposed the Persian Gulf War, but

George Bush, an active Episcopalian, nevertheless waged it. Bill Clinton met constant attack on religious terms from Christians who opposed his tolerant views on abortion, homosexuality, and many more issues as being a denial of the Southern Baptist faith he professes, and he also ran afoul of many religious leaders by refusing to ban the use of land mines.

From the reactions to these presidents and their religious expression and influence, it is clear that some elements of the public's political commitment have colored their interpretations of the religion of a chief executive. The two Southern Baptists, Carter and Clinton, may have been among the most religious and most biblically informed presidents of the century, but various Southern Baptists constantly and vehemently attacked them. In effect, the presidents were seen not as church members but as individuals carrying their faith—badly, their enemies said—into politics.

Dealing with Pluralism

Just as church leaders and elected officials often disagree, the religious public servant may experience inner theological conflict in trying to reconcile personal faith with the nation's pluralism. In a nation where more than 80 percent of the people regard Jesus as a revelation of God, specific witness to Jesus among chief executives carrying out their duties is nonetheless rare, and most people see it as being out of place. Jimmy Carter might have taught orthodox Christology at Sunday school during his years in the White House, but he used more generalized God language in public. He made no mention of his born-again faith in Jesus in his inaugural and very rarely in his public utterances. Elected officials may indeed draw on the ethical impulses at the core of their personal faith, but making such appeals explicit risks offending large numbers of citizens. Political administration is made easier when invocations of faith remain general.

Public officials find themselves in especially sticky situations when policies run counter to their personal religious convictions.

A dramatic instance of this occurred in 1912, when the near-pacifist William Jennings Bryan became secretary of state. Faced with the possibility of war with Germany in 1915, Bryan resigned rather than prepare the troops for what he thought was an unwarranted conflict. In contemporary America, elected officials who are pro-life sometimes find they must allow legally for abortions. Or politicians may find themselves seeking office in a state that legalizes the death penalty while their faith tradition may witness against capital punishment. The public wants its officials to be moral, informed by religious faith, but they don't want that faith to be made particular in a way that conflicts with the officials' execution of their public duties.

Governor Mario Cuomo reflected on this in a speech at Notre Dame in 1984. He addressed a familiar dilemma: he was called to approve or veto legislation on abortion. In his private and churchly world, he opposed abortion. But he was sworn to comply with the laws of the land and, when administering, to take into consideration the interests of the citizenry, the majority of which would have disagreed with his position. Needless to say, his rationale infuriated antiabortion Catholics, who argued that there can be no such split between the private and the public believer and citizen.[4] Yet those not on the ideological front lines of the abortion issue had no difficulty picturing how such a tearing at conscience so regularly occurs in the political realm.

Legislators

The very visible instances of tension between political roles and personal, often religiously based visions belong to government executives, where everything comes down to the voice and vetoing or approving action of a mayor, a governor, a president. Yet in the legislative realm, that conflict is more constant and tense.

The smaller the body of voters who elect representatives—for example, to a town board—the more focused will be pressures and discontents directed toward policymakers and lawmakers. In the United States Congress, the legislatures represent much larger, more complex, and more conflicted constituencies. Still, only the visibility and the scale are different on these varying levels. The issue remains the same.

And that issue is this: What happens when a person is called to make a decision that will be approved by constituents and can be seen as a public good but violates the lawmaker's own faith commitment? Or conversely, what if an elected legislator brings to office a faith commitment, perhaps one whose implications were not known by the voters, that prevents the lawmaker from adequately representing the people who did the electing?

The lines here are not neat; electorates are notoriously or creatively divided among at least two parties and any number of interests, and no lawmaker can respond to and satisfy all. Still, the will of the majority of the represented does get known, thanks to polls, letters, and the media. And sometimes the representative goes against it. Doesn't such a situation lead to ambiguity and then to moral deadening among the hardy?

We are at a classic point that relates to the whole legislative and representative process. And when one introduces religious belief, the point only sharpens. Certainly, the vast majority of lawmakers' decisions are not of the sort that causes lawmakers to reach into the deepest recesses and resources of their ethics. The town board deliberates: Who should get the paving contract? Do we defer a bond issue for another year? Will we plant more trees on the parkway? These decisions do not plumb moral depths. But laws concerning who should live and die (the terminally ill? the deformed fetus?) and who should have access to health care and how to serve justice in appropriations—these decisions require profound resources.

One could say, "Park your religious beliefs at the door." One could say, and often does, "For the sake of the common good, work these things out in private and in your conscience, but when you enter the public arena, remember that you are serving more than yourself." Most do say that overreligiosifying every political decision can soon grow wearying for those who have to hear about it all the time—to the point that both the religion and the policy will suffer.

About this, several things can be said. First, during a campaign, disclosure of the bases of a candidate's ethical outlook can be useful to the voters. But we must keep in mind that we elect people in a "package deal." It is not likely that any of us will agree with all that one elected official does; it is not likely that all the person's moves will be predictable before an election and before the candidate becomes enmeshed in the experience of legislating and facing party discipline. Nor is it ever likely that all constituents will agree with all the decisions any particular elected representative will make.

Second, most of the time, a politician can make decisions on grounds that the secular world would call rational. That is, the agent in politics is not elected as an embodiment of a particular faith community; if this were the case, it would complicate dealing with the whole body whose interests are getting addressed through legislation. We elect someone because she is a conservative Republican, not because she is Mormon, for instance. We expect to know what that person stands for and have some sense of how it would play in the midst of pluralistic choice, though we have to be ready for surprises. Still, tradition and prudence suggest to most people that the overtly religious are to restrain themselves from publicly evoking God and the eccentricities of one faith community when arguing and voting. Claim too often that you vote as you do because you are following the precepts of the Qur'an or the pope, and you will find most voters abandoning you to your devices and fleeing the scene.

Let it be said, third, that the creative legislator still gaining experience has to be free to make some changes, beginning in his or her own mind. Many people elected to village boards or a state senate have not had long experience dealing with constituency and conscience.

Finally, the political arena is not a place where everything will be absolute, neat, and pleasing. No one should run for town board or the House of Representatives expecting to win everything and to deal with cases that are always congruent with the legislator's philosophy at its depth or theology at its broadest. A person who too regularly cuts the corners of conscience will become soulless, dispirited, and, one imagines, eager to go into another line of work or to be rejected by the electorate. In the end, one does not expect to resolve the issue of when an elected official should represent people against his or her personal philosophy and when the theology of cause and conscience match. Airing the issues and ethical roots that give rise to legislation past, present, or future—while it can be overdone and can become a play for votes—is preferable to suppressing them, disguising them, or going against them, even in an imperfect world. And the voter being represented does well to bring strong convictions to bear on an issue but also to realize that legislators will not always have their way, nor will their consciences always be acted on directly and immediately.

Judges

Judges obviously must deal with religion in the thousands of cases involving church property, religious freedom, and related issues. But religion plays a more subtle role in other legal situations as well. In sentencing, judges sometimes deal with the religiously tinged question of conversion and reform: Does this individual show signs of remorse and potential for rehabilitation?

We are aware, for instance of law professors, consultants to judges, who have studied the tradition of formally including "mercy" in the administration of "justice." They consult historical examples to see in what circumstances there is a good bet that society will be better off if a guilty person, for extenuating circumstantial reasons, can be dealt with more generously. In what circumstances is it necessary to exact the full measure of punishment? How a judge assesses the scene, the person before him, and then makes the judgment is colored by his or her views of human nature, as these are professed in a particular religious tradition. A soft judge who administers "cheap grace" and "forgives" the criminal does not serve justice. A hard judge who never recognizes a possibility for redemption in a convicted person may satisfy the law but violate religious injunctions.

Religion may also be a factor when judges consider certain dissenters: if lawbreaking in a particular instance is based on appeal to a "higher law," should it be treated differently from "ordinary" violations? For example, a judge believes, on scriptural grounds, in the legitimacy of providing sanctuary for refugees. What can he or she do in cases where churches have appealed to a higher law, broken the law of the land, and provided illegal sanctuary? The answer: administer the law of the land or resign for conscience's sake. For our legal system to work, a judge's individual religious conscience cannot easily come into play. A judge who happens to be a pacifist must nevertheless enforce laws that make it difficult to avoid military service. A judge who supports animal rights must, regardless of any religious motivations, jail activists who break the laws in that area. Judges who become troubled at administering laws that violate their religious beliefs either have to continue to administer justice while hoping that legislators will change the laws or else step down. A judge, like any other citizen, may believe in a "higher law," but American courts are creatures not of the Bible or the Qur'an but of the U.S. Constitution.

Quite properly, judges are guided entirely by the law of the land. They are not free to transgress legal boundaries on the basis of religious sympathies. Yet they may be moved by the witness of plaintiffs who find themselves in civil difficulty because of actions based in religiously informed conscience. Indeed, it is in the judiciary that the tension between individual conscience and public duty may be most intense.

It is hard to picture any judge, called on to administer in detail a body of law shaped by legislators of many persuasions through decades, if not centuries, finding that everything congruent with that body of law is congruent with his or her religious convictions as well. The law may call for harsh punishments in cases where the judge finds reason to rule more mercifully, but the judge has no choice but to follow the law, regardless of his or her religious outlook. A judge who has come, on religious grounds, to believe that physician-assisted suicide can be a merciful procedure is not free to permit a physician guilty of complicity to go unpunished where the law forbids such measures.

A judge in Alabama, following his born-again faith, may insist on posting the Ten Commandments on his courthouse wall and flouting decisions of the United States Supreme Court. But unless the law and the Supreme Court interpretations change, he will be at least in technical violation of the law he is sworn to serve, and continuing to do so will undercut the majesty of law in the name of what others consider a sectarian understanding and witness. Of course, one measure of discipline and control in all these processes is the fact that judges do not like to be overruled by higher courts.

Individuals Energized by Their Religious Beliefs: A Sign of Hope for the Republic

The character of highly religious and ethical individuals may predispose them to purism and absolutism. They may wish that all their acts and the acts of elected and appointed officials in a civil society could be congruent with their beliefs. Some may believe that these acts can be and have to be because such beliefs are grounded in their grasp of divine revelation, church law, or natural law. Yet in an imperfect world and in a pluralistic society where many wills and interests seek expression and many interpretations of truth and justice collide, it will not be possible for the "pure" and the "absolute" to win out all or even most of the time.

Awareness of this reality should produce realism in the minds and intentions of the thoughtful. However, the same realization does not provide an excuse for the citizen-believer to withdraw from politics. Such awareness is not to be a barrier against the resolves of an individual to make witness heard and to have effect in the civil order.

Being paralyzed by the sense of limits on how one's beliefs can be implemented is destructive of common good in a republic. Being energized by an awareness of possibilities based on one's beliefs and their effects is a sign of hope for improvement in that republic.

4

The Political Power of
Traditional Institutions

*Thesis: Traditional institutions—congregations,
denominations, and ecumenical agencies—provide
an effective public voice for religious people.*

For a moment, assume that you are a member of a congregation in a denomination that belongs to an ecumenical council. You did not join these communities to find a political outlet; parties are for that. So are caucuses, causes, movements, and agencies. They exist for politics.

Religious communities, with few exceptions, tend to spread wider nets and may include Republicans and Democrats, leftists and rightists, passive and active people, some focused on the life to come and others using the religious message to change this world.

Religious bodies, however, exist in a political world. Many of their intentions occur where they bump into political forces. In a way, they are anomalies in the political world—a fact that makes them attractive to some politicians and problematic to others.

Take the Southern Baptist Convention, the nation's largest Protestant body. By its own description, it is highly congregational. The local church is the unit that God has ordained. From there on, everything is a matter of choice and prudence. The fact that it was born fifteen years before the Civil War reveals, however, that political instances were part of the heredity of the denomination.

Often it saw itself or was criticized by others as being so other-worldly that it did not notice politics. It might train individuals to be responsible citizens, but it stayed out of politics. On occasion, its state or national conventions might speak up and organize forces, as some of them did to promote Prohibition or to oppose the electoral campaign of Catholic Al Smith in 1928.

When the civil rights movement gained momentum in the 1950s, however, a commission of the convention began to speak to the thousands of Southern Baptist churches and somehow to speak for them, with politics in mind. It was time to change laws that kept blacks from access to political power and to ensure their other rights. The action went against the sentiment and practice of many Southern Baptist individuals and churches. Yet the Christian Life Commission found reason to testify on this and other matters, most notably on separation of church and state on Capitol Hill.

As the culture and the convention changed, the Christian Life Commission came under the control of conservatives who had their own agenda. Again, because "messengers" from the churches elected the president and the president had enormous appointing powers and the appointers picked people of a particular persuasion, one can say that the Christian Life Commission was a fairly representative agency for the membership majority.

When the commission speaks out and organizes lobbies against legislation that promotes choice in respect to abortions, the commission whips itself into action. The individual member may feel unrepresented and left out or put out. But the act of quitting the Southern Baptist Convention for reasons of politics demands spiritual energies and sets of priorities that belong only to the few.

It becomes important for sophisticated politicians to determine or sense just how representative the voice of the annual convention or the perennial commission is. How many votes are there in those who say they represent "Southern Baptists"? If the leadership has succeeded in helping mold the disparate forces into a kind of united voice, it will have power in Congress—a fact that nettles the minority on any issue in the convention.

The Origins of Traditional Religious Institutions

During its multicentury experiment with religious freedom, the United States has developed a number of organizational forms simply by adapting chiefly European patterns. In the Europe that the colonists left behind, churches were *established*, which meant that they were supported by law, privileged, and largely paid for out of public funds. Several nations provided some measure of religious freedom. For example, Catholic France allowed for some Protestant life, and Presbyterian Scotland included some Anglican and Catholic parishes, Baptist congregations, and Quaker meetings. Countries with established religions tolerated others grudgingly, but they did provide a limited amount of religious freedom.

Of course, congregations and parishes were there, but ordinarily they were creatures of government or had to conform to boundaries and policies set by governments. These forms were seen as traditional, deeply rooted, and not in need of revision. So when Catholics came to New Spain and New France, they brought with them the habits of establishment and wanted simply to transplant the monopolist system of parishes under government control. In similar fashion, the Separatists and Puritans who settled most of New England set themselves up with privilege and tax support, imitating the very church they had left England to avoid. In most of the southern colonies, Anglicanism became the official faith. At the time of the nation's birth, nine of the thirteen colonies maintained some kind of religious establishment. In this situation, to speak of a congregation or a parish made sense, but to locate it in a larger structure called a denomination would have been inaccurate. The denomination itself was only beginning to appear among radicals in the British Isles before 1776.

Denominationalism came in response to disestablishment, which occurred only gradually. The First Amendment to the U.S. Constitution ensured that there would be no nationally established religion, and one by one the new states followed suit. By 1833, all the former colonies guaranteed rights—at least on paper—to the various voluntary religious forms, now usually called denominations. This leveled the playing field, and congregations changed their character. Minority faiths could now organize publicly. Jews no longer huddled in ghettos but gathered together in synagogues, often called congregations. Catholics preferred the spatial language of "parish," but the actual form it took was that of the congregation. And even as they integrated congregations into larger structures in various ways, all Protestants organized themselves into congregations. Collective groupings of congregations began to behave together in denominations.

Religious Institutions: Do They Have a Place on the Political Scene?

The majority of Americans do not vote in most elections. Often a tiny minority stirs itself to elect school boards and town boards. Many citizens are so alienated from politics as now practiced that they do not want to see any of it introduced in churches. For many, synagogue or church represents a haven in a hostile world. Why introduce political arguments that may not affect the political order but will disturb the peace and quiet of those who had come for sanctuary and prayer?

Meanwhile, politicians often find that most congregations and denominations are not the most politically unified organizations. A sizable group like the United Methodist Church or the Presbyterian Church may speak out on the plight of migrant workers, but the religious activists who shape those denominational voices may be a minority. The legislator may never meet any Methodists or Presbyterians who hold those views. So why should a politician focus on a denomination or congregation when it would be more politically efficient to meet activists in other strictly political forums? Denominations and congregations often embody a diversity of opinion and energy that complicates a politician's efforts to deal with predictable, unified constituencies.

Budding politicians might find good reason to overlook or even sneer at religious institutions. "How many divisions has the pope?" Joseph Stalin was reputed to have said, demeaning the supposed power of Catholicism in the face of the state's military might. Politicians are known to be on good terms with certain constituencies: unions, management organizations, feminist groups, elderly advocates. Through such organizations, politicians can tap into wells of organized support, and they run the risk of powerful opposition if these constituencies are ignored. At the beginning of the twenty-first century, is there enough power in religious institutions to warrant political engagement with the spiritual and its institutional houses?

It turns out that the pope does have some weapons with dramatic political consequences. Though it might seem that traditional religious organizations have few or no troops, it would be a mistake to ignore the residual political potential of religious institutions. Their political power may have waned in the twentieth century, but congregations, denominations, and ecumenical agencies remain potentially powerful locations for religious citizens to express a collective political voice.

We will use three different lenses to explore the role of religious institutions; more precisely, we will examine agencies of three different scales—congregations, denominations, and federations—using an appropriate lens for each.

Most people who express their spiritual responses in a community do so through local congregations. The word *congregation* may not be common to all faiths; Roman Catholics, for instance, speak of *parishes* and reserve the word *congregation* for religious orders (monks and nuns), and Episcopalians also prefer *parish*. Non-Christian faiths often have terms of their own, though Jews and most Protestants are at home with this one.

We will use *congregation* to refer to any group of people gathered around a common scripture, belief, message, or intention in a given locale. The communal energies of most believers get put to work through congregations. When they express themselves politically, the impulse and output reflect person-to-person wrestling over issues.

The word *denomination* has to cover realities as different as the Muslim *ummah*, Christian *church*, for many Christians *confession*, and countless other variations. Some "churches" do not like to think of themselves as denominations, and some of them call others "sects." But no matter how sensitively a social scientist or reporter handles these nuances, they all get registered mentally as denominations.

The denomination is a translocal reality, a connection, made somehow among congregations that share a faith and intention in broad outline. Some groups consider the denomination nothing more than a practical arrangement by which congregations, remaining "autonomous," find common cause, enlarge their scope, and become responsible to each other. For others, the denomination as "confession," or creedally united body, takes precedence and finds expression in local congregations. Whatever the internal interpretation, politically it is the denomination that wrestles with issues, takes stands, promotes policies, and holds sway in the public eye, even if its national positions are less reflective of the daily life of adherents in all the local bodies. Thus to a lawmaker, for instance, the denominational voice is heard more regularly than the congregational one, but this voice is not necessarily expressive of the entire membership. Thanks to the dynamics of how bureaucracies are perpetuated, task forces appointed, positions debated, and votes cast at national assemblies of denominations, the viewpoints and workings of the denomination may end up being quite unrepresentative of the membership. Still, in most religious groups, delegates and officers are elected, so they can be assumed to reflect at least some sentiment of the membership. And where they are appointed, as in Catholicism, the effective ones, however "prophetic" or "intransigent" they may be, have to be in some sort of harmony with the people they serve, or they will not serve credibly.

The word *ecumenical* comes from the Greek for "inhabited world" and has come to mean not only some sort of spiritual reality that crosses or underlies denominations and confessions but also the actual working out of common purpose and elements of common faith beyond the denominations. Thus there may be local, state, regional, and world councils of Christian churches. The churches, not the individual members, constitute these often rather loose federations. For that reason, the policies and procedures may be out of step with what an individual member or congregation may wish to express politically. Yet the ecumenical agency does provide ways for believers to include viewpoints larger than what the local might teach them. To speak of religious interests in human rights is very different for congregations in the United States when they become aware of the histories and needs and interests of fellow believers who exist under totalitarian regimes, where political opportunity is limited—and vice versa.

To the press and in national and international politics, the ecumenical position is most accessible. If the national or world council speaks, it conveys a certain kind of authority. At the same time, savvy observers have learned that the pronouncements of ecumenical bodies may be quite remote in sentiment and theology from what one finds in local churches, and its actual authority to effect change is limited. In this book, *ecumenical* refers not to independent voluntary associations but to groups that in a way supersede the individual because his or her congregation, through a denomination, is a member. Someone who persistently disagrees with the politics of a voluntary association can work to change it or simply walk away. It is harder for a committed Presbyterian to abandon an ecumenical organization if his or her denomination is a member of an interdenominational council.

We will therefore use the close-up lens for the congregation, the middle-distance one for the denomination, and the telescope for the ecumenical council or federation.

The Congregation

In his book *Cosmopolis*, Stephen Toulmin, a noted philosopher of science, ends by speaking of some paradoxes of modernity.[1] One of them has to do with the surprising survival and recovery of the local in a cosmopolitan era. That is, as corporate life and mass communications grow ever larger and more efficient and as the globe shrinks into a network more connected than a neighborhood once was, this connecting is partial and deals only with some aspects of life. Many people face this bureaucratization and corporateness by "digging in" and paying attention to their "tribe," their actual neighborhood. They crave community and find it not through the people to whom they are "wired" over the Internet or with whom they make up an audience for television. They find that they can ward off some forces of modernity that they consider dehumanizing and can hold on to old power and find new power through local entities.

In the religious world, this means that the congregation has retained a hold on most community-bound believers and has even taken on new power as mistrust of translocal and less immediate bodies, such as the denomination, have for various reasons waned in influence. The congregation is not the only local expression: the precinct, the mall, and the voluntary association all deal with strictly local issues. The congregation meets rough competition among bidders for loyalty. Adherents owe or yield part of their hearts and much of their scheduled time to nonreligious local phenomena. Yet the congregation remains, and although it may appear less prominently on lists of citizen priorities than at various other times in history, it remains a key focus for religious energies. Statistics on religious participation and financial support of religion back this up: the congregation is by far the most effective and most vital way in which religious people gather themselves and their resources together.[2]

The makeup of American religious congregational forces has changed in recent decades. Local African American churches were and remain in politics, but there have been upheavals on other fronts. Catholic parishes, for instance, cannot be counted on simply to reflect the political and economic positions of the bishops, who issue most of the Catholic position papers on social and other public issues. The most vivid illustration in the minds of non-Catholics in politics today is the gap between the position of the Vatican and the National Conference of Catholic Bishops, on the one hand, and the practices of American Catholics "down the street," on the other, with respect to birth control and various policies in health care institutions. Official Catholicism has a reasoned and regularly expressed position prohibiting "artificial" birth control, meaning all forms except the "natural" method. The hundreds of hospitals in the Catholic Health Association (CHA) must live by "directives" that reflect this position.

At the same time, most American Catholics are quite forthright about their disagreement with this position. Although they may not be able to change the policies of CHA member hospitals, they may well seek out health care institutions that permit procedures and practices that the official statements do not. Catholics on public hospital boards may feel free to establish policies there that are different from the church position and to expound on what the official position means to them.

For much of the century after 1918, when the Catholic bishops issued a "program" for social policy, the gap between formal and local expression was probably largest with respect to labor unions. Overall, the church sought to give a voice to the labor movement, especially to unions, as a working out of policies issued from the Vatican as early as 1891. Much of the American workforce was Catholic, and these pro-labor views were very congenial, supportive, and supported. But many Catholic parishes included middle-class and some upper-class members who were leaders in management. They may have given some moment's attention to the bishops' utterances, if only to have a twinge of conscience or to get ammunition for resisting or even fighting back. They set labor policies on terms quite independent of the bishops' statements.

The greatest change at the congregational level, however, may have come about on the Protestant front. Four decades ago, the congregations belonging to the so-called mainstream in Protestantism—Congregationalists turned United Church of Christ, Presbyterians, Episcopalians, Disciples of Christ, Baptists of the North, United Methodists, most kinds of Lutherans and Reformed—reflected positions of their national denominations on the local scene. But denominations as voices have weakened, and their power has become uncertain. More, not less, of the position taking and political action among mainstream Protestantism has fallen (or risen) to the parish level. The congregation works with less of a denominational protective blanket on social themes, or it breaks with denominational policies more freely because the word from headquarters or the assemblies counts for less.

Meanwhile, in a great reversal, the congregations in the evangelical sector—Pentecostals, fundamentalists, evangelicals, Southern Baptists, Missouri Synod Lutherans, the Christian Reformed—have reconceived and reconfigured their power situations. Once content to use this power to preserve their own tax exemptions or zoning ordinances, they have begun to take a very public stand on a range of issues. It is more likely for a fundamentalist congregation to picket a clinic where abortions are performed than for a mainstream Protestant church to join an antigambling crusade. Local churches intervene on local hospital policies. They may be the most active critics of policy at local school board and library board meetings. A mother may hear a report that a book in the public school library expresses views on homosexuality or human sexuality that offend her. She examines the book and alerts other parents who belong to the same congregation. They find that by getting the support of their minister, who can use the pulpit against the offending book, and their congregation, which they can easily reach, they amass power they would not otherwise have. Soon the local Baptist church is hailed for speaking up in areas where the larger Baptist denomination does not have occasion, time, or impetus. This agitation on school and library boards is one of the most immediate expressions of politics. It may lead to electing of different school boards, but by and large the politicking stops short of the actual voting booth.

Often the stands taken by the local churches are just that: locally based and dealing with local issues. An evangelical congregation may as often as not deviate from National Association of Evangelical (NAE) policy stands, though this deviation would be less marked than in the other three denominational settings we have just described. Leaders of the NAE caution that the public at large is getting a misrepresentative view owing to the high profile of the more radical right. Many of the evangelical congregations have programs that outstrip those of the mainstream when it comes to care for the environment, the poor, and the victims of injustice. It becomes ever harder to count on congregations to be in line with a single denominational policy and also harder to predict the ways in which a local church, often under the influence of the pastor, chooses political positions.

Others note that local evangelical churches are often more autonomous than other assemblies; they are more ready than others to insist that no one represents them, though they may show more deference than others to local pastors. So the local pastor becomes a very visible agent and exemplar to the larger community, beginning with the home congregation. If the pastor becomes too political, especially on a controversial issue not near the congregation's heart, resistance will arise. In many of these congregations, "preaching politics from the pulpit" may doom a pastor, even one who is merely espousing positions expressed by denominational representatives.

In many parts of the country, the local congregations of prominent churches once served as a kind of unofficial establishment. But now, due to the gradual disappearance of religious studies from public schools, increasing pluralism, the absence of religious imagery in the mass media, and the decline of families and congregations as nurturing agents, the vocabulary based on what had once been a

"Christian memory" is disappearing. For example, Baptists with memories going back to colonial New England will recall that any policy that favored the established church or faiths other than their own was regarded as a suppression of their liberties by the government. Roger Williams, whom they often revered as the pioneer Baptist, cut the cross out of the royal flag flying over Salem in the Plymouth colony early in the seventeenth century. By the late twentieth century, many who claimed the heritage of Williams and the Baptists had totally reversed themselves. They fought against the American Civil Liberties Union or others who wanted to remove crosses from town flags and logos. They wanted it as part of displays on courthouse lawns. They were now moved less by Baptist memory than by contemporary evangelical culture, more alarmed by the threat of godlessness than by God allied with Crown.

Those who do remain with congregations have less tradition on which to draw and are more at the mercy of those who represent current issues effectively on whatever grounds. For instance, it is often pointed out that the Southern Baptist Convention and its congregations of more nearly fundamentalist stripe often reflect generic fundamentalist viewpoints, as promoted in televangelism or by groups like the Christian Coalition, than they reflect historic Baptist outlooks. This may lead politicians to be ever more alert listeners and effective interpreters of what they hear from local congregations.

When analysts discuss congregations as political agencies, they find themselves almost instinctively slipping away to discussion of denominational, ecumenical, and other transcongregational institutions. Is this fact not revealing? This indicates that congregations should be seen less as islands and more as elements in complex ecologies and milieux. If legislators do not become adept at listening critically to the voices of congregations, however much more difficult it is to hear such voices than those of interest groups or denominational bureaucracies, they will miss some of the more representative and immediate endeavors to relocate religion in the political order.

When we speak of representativeness and immediacy, this is only to note that congregations embody and express values. These values may not match those of the large church bodies to which they belong, but that does not mean that they are not value-laden or inspired. Congregations' faithfulness to their own value orientation is what often surprises the public. A person may be a member of a conservative congregation in which managers predominated and the pro–labor union policies of a denomination were rarely mentioned. Then a neighborhood situation changes and there is suddenly support for labor unions—support again based in the norms of a church body's heritage but reflective of new values born of new situations. The urban map changes constantly. Majestic edifices, their brass railings and Tiffany windows remaining to remind new inhabitants of the glory days when wealthy managers built and endowed the churches, come to serve blue-collar communities. The new membership is not a bit interested in adhering to what the founders in the era of the Rockefellers and Morgans and Vanderbilts advocated. They look for ways in which the religious message can be supportive of them in labor organization. If they are Christian, they will adhere to the same scriptures, but now different portions will be emphasized, and the old rationales will be altered, forgotten, or rejected.

Congregations may often be perceived as agents of stasis, but on some levels they adapt quickly and in nuanced ways. Thus they serve as indicators of popular opinion, still somehow reflective of traditions that thrive beyond the local community.

Let's look at the various roles congregations play.

Providing Services No Longer Provided by Political Programs

Though they rarely think of themselves as primarily political, congregations nevertheless affect the *polis*—the human city and its political centers—in myriad ways. In recent years, congregations have often been challenged to fill various gaps left due to a decline of governmental support. When they do address these gaps, they enter politics even as voluntary agencies. Why? To observers who prefer more government involvement in welfare funding, the congregation that is doing the addressing may retard efforts to reinstitute "the welfare state." The congregation that does not respond to the call to fill the gap may be seen as too supportive of such a welfare society.

So a congregation may establish a homeless shelter and ministry and please those who see its services as alleviating the homeless situation. Critics may regard this as a meager stopgap response, no substitute for tax-supported work. Yet the congregation, acting on its faith, says that it cannot wait for the political process to resolve complex issues: there are people nearby who need a roof tonight! Their leaders and members have seen the need, deployed their rarely ample resources, listened to and spoken for the newcomers, and helped change the demographic fabric and hence the politics of the nation. There is political power in such activities, even when no one beyond local congregations has been involved. Members who support homeless shelters may think that they are merely doing what voluntary associations have always done. But what they do either calls attention to the need for more tax-supported approaches to problems or gets justified as an alternative that makes tax support less necessary. The involvement of voluntary associations as political may not always be apparent at the time. But historians have a perspective that shows how different these matters look in retrospect. Thus at the turn of the twentieth century, the Salvation Army in its local branches very effectively dealt with victims of sudden industrial change. An employer could lay off hundreds of striking workers, and the Salvation Army would be there to minister to the unemployed. But those actions were later seen as either having made it more difficult for Social Gospel politics, which supported labor unions, to make its way or having given visibility to situations that cried for legislative change.

Because the spheres of church and state collide in every such incident or development, guardians of the line between them find themselves either conceding to intrusions or vigorously opposing them. If today's Salvation Army, for all the money it raises as a voluntary association, is a main agent dispersing tax funds to face human need, alerted citizens ask, will this bond with the state give privilege and advantage to one faith—for the Salvation Army is also a denomination—and will those who take care of the needs of the body resist temptations to use their access to those in need as an opportunity for evangelism or privileged ministry?

Conversely, can one be so vigilant in opposing spiritual ministry in such situations that fine points of church-state doctrine get debated while people suffer and even die? That these musings are expressed as questions indicates that we are dealing with an unresolved area in national life and public religion.

Providing Variety

We do not get much opportunity to help formulate policy for the World Council of Churches or the National Conference of Catholic Bishops or the Central Conference of American Rabbis unless we are elected to one of these bodies. But we may be a Republican who joins a congregation with strong Democratic tendencies in politics. The congregation was not organized to be sympathetic to the Democrats, but it nevertheless reflects partisan views. We may be a new suburbanite, uprooted from a city congregation where pro-labor views predominated and now a member of a "management" church. We may have moved to an area where retired military people unite as United Methodists in a congregation, and they will support policies that advance defense spending or local zoning that permits enlargement of military facilities. Yet we may bring a near-pacifist voice to the congregation. The majority and we, with our minority, cannot pretend that the other does not exist. But in casual encounters, classes, response to sermons, and formulating policy, we stand a chance of hearing each other and changing our opinions to reflect the views of the other in a way the denomination or council cannot.

Of course, listening to divergent opinions is not always a gentle experience. The local congregation can become the embodiment of polarities, of factions, of us-versus-them feelings that can be unsettling and may even lead some members to move to other congregations. Or it may mean that opposing interests reach some rough equilibrium and find harmony at worship but still find it difficult to agree on positions and actions in the political realm. Town hall will be much less interested in dealing with political issues concerning First Church's desire to build a residence for mildly retarded adults in a residential community if its members are evenly split on the issue. This complication does, however, lend weight to the town hall discussion and make the deliberations more real and less abstract.

Disagreement among congregational elements and factions may be so fractious, intense, and unpleasant that permanent minorities may weary of being unrepresented or misrepresented in a congregation's actions and may feel obliged to move on. People switch loyalties all the time. This shifting among congregations has to be seen as yet another form of realignment and thus of political expression, even when it does not go by that name. We know of a suburban community church that several decades ago prospered by attracting as members physicians from another congregation who were reacting against preachments and policy statements by their church's pastors, who supported "socialized medicine." Such shifts may be demoralizing for congregational leadership (or welcomed by the churches receiving the refugees), but they must be recognized as political forces.

In the Presbyterian congregations in some southern locales during the civil rights movement, some pastors and lay leaders encouraged their congregations to be hospitable to "outside agitators" by welcoming and sheltering northerners who came to help register voters. Unapproving of that stance, large numbers of members in many of these churches moved off to help organize new Presbyterian congregations or denominations or joined local Baptist or other churches less hospitable to the idea. These were very vivid political expressions on the part of people who would say they were simply living out the implications of the prophets and the gospels.

We may be giving the wrong impression here, as if suggesting that congregations came together to be political agencies. Most of the time people go about worshiping, enjoying fellowship, and engaging in works of mercy unmoved by political storms around them. At other times, they may do their politicking quietly, so as not to be seen as intruding on lines separating church and state or so as not to alienate people they would like to attract or hold as members. In such cases, politicians have to be alert to catch the nuances and subtleties. By and large, they become good at that and learn to know which congregation will knock on their door and when.

Various polls will ask local church members whether they rely on their faith when it comes to social and political issues. Most will say they do, on matters such as the death penalty, homosexuality, and abortion. But faith-based norms do not show up much on issues of race, poverty, the environment, and justice. Sometimes this failure to reflect official viewpoints results less from resistance than from ignorance. It is often reported that local parish priests may never publicize what they read in the bishops' letters. This is not always because they oppose them but rather because they have other duties and agendas and give a low priority to such proclamations.

Furthering Education and Discussion

Now and then a major ethical thinker—we have Paul Ramsey in mind—will write a book that questions who speaks for the churches or attacks the churches for acting as if they can speak for members.[3] In response, many local churches have been careful to say that they use materials that speak "to" the churches. Most denominations have policy statements on abortion, in vitro fertilization, cessation of medical treatment, and the like. They get formulated by theologians and people on the front lines in these fields. Thus the Catholic bishops' letters on nuclear warfare or the economy became textbooks in parishes where many members had not given thought to the issue or who had not had their positions theologically informed. The writers of these statements do not always win majority consent of congregants who use the materials or study the pronouncements. But these publications do become teaching devices, and as minds get changed, they have political effect.

Not that congregational action always results from the unanimous and wholehearted support of the whole membership of congregations. Politicians are confused by the many dividing lines over policy that run not only between but through congregations.

What good is it, some ask, if factions and congregations virtually cancel each other out over political stands? If both elements in a congregation quote from the same scripture, stand in the same theological tradition, and intend to be equally moral, how should the politician and other citizens react? There are no easy answers to such questions. But most advocates of congregational involvement would say that at the very least the quickening of interest and passion within congregations may lead to learning opportunities. Members have to reconfront ancient and normative sacred texts and try to interpret them in conscience. Subsequently, everyone is better off with such responses than with the apathy and indifference that might otherwise characterize such a gathering.

The already mentioned approaches by congregations often find support in written testimonies that clarify and call for further support of many political causes. In most denominations, congregational representatives vote on social policy at churchwide convocations. Whether or not they were all represented at such assemblies, particular congregations then have to exemplify and act on or resist such resolutions. When denominations were more powerful institutions and congregants were less informed or less suspicious than they are today, and when the political world may have seemed slightly more innocent, denominations often gave the impression that their declarations spoke for millions of members and—politicians take note—voters. In recent years, the resolutions and statements from assemblies or denominational agencies are accorded far less respect.

Even if they are seen as less than fully representative and not having much clout, denominational resolutions have acquired a new function: they have become teaching devices. They sometimes arise out of questions posed by congregational situations. Task forces, agencies, bureaus, and delegates to assemblies then deal with them, and eventually they are brought up for vote and sent back to the local churches.

Often the process is too slow to have much effect. Many Jews were disappointed that Christian denominations did not speak up to rally support for Israel during the Six-Day War of 1967. What they did not realize was that in most Christian denominations, no one had been authorized to speak for the congregations and adherents; people could only express personal views and then speak to members in and through their congregations. And even at the end of the slow and deliberate process, ordinarily not everyone is convinced by or in agreement with a policy, even when it claims to be based on normative scriptures. The new Presbyterian Confession of Faith released in 1967 included, along with doctrinal declarations, critiques of certain military and defense policies, statements that were opposed by many prominent Presbyterians. Those who seek reform on the institutionally religious front regularly urge that the congregation-denomination-congregation cycle be streamlined and speeded up.

Many of the claims for political hearing do not seem to be derived from anything specifically theological, meaning the Bible, traditions, or the theological or confessional heritage. They are in any case proclaimed as being rooted somewhere beyond the prejudices of most people who hold them at the moment. Here the interaction of politician and pastors or people can serve as educational activities for both, as the religious and political groups alike struggle to redefine themselves, their place, their language, and their roles. One of the impressive regular counsels mentioned at this point of interaction has to do with basic adult education. Congregants ask, What are we and what do we believe? How do we connect our theology with our practice? Such questions come up less frequently in the abstract of congregational coffee talk than they do when the larger public poses them to the otherwise relatively enclosed group.

These values often become realized not just in what passes for theological inquiry in most parishes but also in agendas, vision and mission statements, and belief systems in the larger world. Believers' values may become manifest less in detailed theologies than in employment agencies, job training, or available day care. Yet when pressed, most religious people will move beyond mere duty and goodwill and at least try to locate their motivations in a larger theological context. To do this effectively, believers may have to do some homework to learn and teach what resources are available and potentially attractive for articulating their core values.

Providing the Power of the Prophetic Word

Most people do not join most congregations to be politically moved all the time. Yet most of them do so with some sort of belief that they should respond to the scriptures and messages that reach them there. These speak to the heart and have immediate applications in ways that even the most efficient mass media of communications cannot. The modern congregational voices do not have a monopoly and may often seem pitifully weak against organized corporate power and political polish, yet they can have a special authenticity and appeal. The pulpit may sometimes be the source of the call, but so can the parish newspaper, presentations by interest groups, the work of committees, and reports on what the congregation has done. All beckon members to "join us in furthering the work."

The power of the pulpit is strong but limited. In congregations not organized around a particular political cause, as most of them are not, the preacher who reduces the message to overt politics will be ineffective and possibly of short tenure. In Jewish or Christian circles, drawing on the political ethics implied in the rural and village worlds of a land far away and long ago does not guarantee that contemporary applications of those texts will always be appropriate in all contexts. "The pulpit" has unfortunately become the code word for much language and action by congregations in the public and political realms. The pulpit is but one instrument, and on it there might well be a sign, "Handle with Care." Many words of a preacher will be heard as reflecting the unique situation of the preacher, who may not be a homeowner, has an education most members do not have, and does not live in the "real world" of the majority of the members.

Does this mean that the preacher should muffle language about social wrongs that need addressing and not point to ways to address them? It would be a violation of the prophetic dimensions of congregational leadership to answer yes. But the prophet's language, originally spoken in theocracies where God ruled through judge or monarch, could be focused and absolute-sounding in ways that are difficult to grasp in a world of democracy, participatory politics, and great complexity. It is one thing for Jeremiah to denounce the rich who preempt the property of others. It is another to address injustices worked on the poor through the savings and loan crisis or when unemployment in a community occurs because of remote corporate takeovers and mergers. Yet not everything that Jeremiah said is irrelevant or inapplicable. To believe that it must be would mean a form of scriptural interpretation that turns a congregation into a historical society, a nostalgia club. In addition to effective action, congregations can also bring unique and refreshing voices into public conversation. Their critiques and analyses may be truly nonpartisan. For religious reasons, congregations are often called to uplift the needs of otherwise overlooked members of society.

Integral to the life of almost every congregation is professional or, in some traditions, ordained pastoral leadership. The pastor can be a key figure in the bearing of politics on religion and vice versa. He or she is the occupational gatekeeper to the world beyond the local parish. The pastor is in fact in a kind of political position with regard to the congregation. Not to push members at all in the name of justice informed by biblical or other such norms is regarded as

compromising. Where, then, does prophecy go? To push congregations too hard and too fast on the same grounds may distract or pre-
occupy congregations and even paralyze some. Where the pastors are
seen as good pastors and meet legitimate needs of the people served,
they gain validity for the positions they take and promote among
congregants. Few pastors would abandon hospital calls or sermon
preparation and administrative tasks to become full-time advocates
of political positions. But many of them would include public and
even political engagements in their larger theological agenda.

Wielding Power in Excess of Numerical Strength

A congregation has its own kind of power, limited though it may
be. When people have long been nurtured with a grasp of the eternal, with appeals that transcend day-to-day politics, with messages
that call them to sacrifice, they will respond differently than they
will when they perceive that nothing but self-serving interests are
at stake. Or they may respond to clerical leaders and fellow congregants who have faithfully served them in crisis in ways they will
not to the politician or agitator of the moment. And even small
congregations can have their voices heard over unorganized community forces or groups that got their way because there was no
opposition.

In some cities, for example, where the number and location of
taverns is open to discussion, poor little local congregations,
through the clarity, focus, and persistence of their members, have
won over enough voters to combat the tavern and liquor interests
or to counter corrupt judges who had once been able to exercise
power without counterforce. Sometimes the energy and witness of
the few can gain power disproportionate to the numbers they directly represent.

Making Size Matter

At the same time, politicians and governmental officials do count
votes. So they pay attention to the potential number of voters a

congregation can influence. The megachurch gains political power by sheer weight of numbers. But many new members may have seen such a congregation as a kind of refuge from public engagement and prefer to make use of its resources for private or family development. There may be so much political variety in such a congregation that it would be hard to begin to introduce social issues there. A congregation of seventy seniors, most of them women, may be so responsive to neighborhood and other needs that they provide a more potent political force than the large ones. At the same time, their life situations will keep them from letting a congregation be reduced to mere political agency and social issues advocate. They can grow so small and weak that they no longer look for much beyond survival and a congregational address to their intimate needs. Or they can find a new mission.

Thoughtfully Stretching Response Time

One feature of congregational life that colors political engagement has to do with temporality. When an issue suddenly appears on a city council or legislative assembly agenda, action on it has to be relatively rapid. Politicians swiftly bargain for position and have to state a clear yes or no on issues and policies. Although congregations are sometimes the agitators who put items on the agenda, they are more likely to be tardy on the scene and may slow down citizen response to specific actions.

As congregations deliberate, attending to multiple perspectives and issues, it may seem that the inherent slowness of the process seems to lead to nothing substantial. However, subtle but eventually significant mind changing goes on, and when it results in new religious motivations, there are strong consequences.

Thus week after week, year after year, preachers may preach in support of positive attitudes on the part of congregants to people who are "other" in race or social class, but they may not make instant converts among their own congregations. But they help inaugurate discussions of the sort that result in durable action.

Interacting Directly with People

Congregations that, alongside their central spiritual and communal work, attend to the political order are able to work out responses in living ways over periods of time—and then begin to act on their responses, since congregations, unlike denominational headquarters, are hands-on, face-to-face agencies.

Those who relish the potential of congregations in this sphere have learned from their parents that congregational action loses effect if it is not grounded in profound features of the worshiping and study life of a congregation. Members are ritual beings, whether of high or low or middling type. And as they enact the liturgies and ceremonies, they can find motifs in which to ground their responses to calls for action. Such grounded responses will have more staying power than those that come from individuals who are unprotected when storms of change come upon them. As their life together issues in action, this will take on concrete forms in ways that more abstract statements or calls for action by denominational agencies do not. These forms appear in congregational life alongside those that express nonpolitical or less overtly political concerns. These might include those attentive to sacramental life, meditation, the works of love, or attempts to nurture a moral life. But their very combination with these other interests and the potential for the diffusion of political proposals make for political actions harder to plot but not less effective than those that result from single-issue causes.

Denominations

Do you find anything strange about the following questions?

- What is the Catholic stand on abortion?

- What is the Muslim attitude toward U.S. Middle East policy?

- What is the Jewish view on school vouchers?

- What does the Southern Baptist Convention think of homosexual rights?

- Have the Lutherans taken a stand on physician-assisted suicide?

- What is the Mormon position on environmental issues in the American West?

- Did the Mennonites oppose the draft?

- Do the United Methodists still oppose gambling?

- Why did the Presbyterians get involved with the issue of refugees and immigration legislation?

Tradition and instinct lead us to ask such questions because so much of American life has been organized along denominational lines. Listings for places of worship in the Yellow Pages are grouped under denominational headings. The *Yearbook of American and Canadian Churches* identifies well over two hundred denominations.

Mention Islam, and you must quickly follow up with reference to what type of Islam you have in mind: Sunni or Shi'ite, African American orthodoxy, Nation of Islam, or some more fundamentalist branch. Similarly, there is no simple Judaism on the political scene: one must deal with Orthodox, Reform, Conservative, and Reconstructionist takes on political statements and efforts—all the while knowing that the Anti-Defamation League or the American Jewish Committee may be more efficient at influencing politics.

This is not to say that all religion is comprehended denominationally. Most of the spirituality that fills the role of religion in the life of many thousands is not classifiable in denominational terms. Nor does the concept of denominational organization do justice to many developing aspects of religious expression. Gays and lesbians may belong to the Universal Fellowship of Metropolitan Community Churches or the Roman Catholic Church, which means they are denominationally differentiated. But on many issues, they have

more in common with each other than with their codenomination-
alists. When political issues predominate and church members need
each other to assert power and seek more, what they hold in common matters more than what they believe particularly. Similarly,
many new devotees of African American religion view it as a cohort,
an element, particularly when issues of political power come up. At
the same time, whoever has dealt with the varieties of African
Methodism, plus the black Baptist or Pentecostal churches, comes
quickly to realize that denominations matter much to members.

Corporate Identity

Denominations work with a variety of polities. Not all ways of governing give equal voice to the memberships.

Polity

A large constituency speaks when the denomination does. The
polity of the various denominations has some bearing on how they
address the political scene in particular and the public arena in general. Hierarchical bodies, at least in theory, grant leaders more central authority. A papal encyclical or episcopal letter is supposed to
have more weight and bearing than issues from congregational bodies. Connectional churches, such as those of Methodist polity, imply
commitments and covenants that are more profound than congregationalist ones. They disseminate what goes on in their general
conventions more efficiently than congregationalists do. And scholars usually describe congregational bodies as least representative on
the denominational level. They have no authority except that
ceded them by the local churches.

Of course, in practice things may work out quite differently. In
Catholic bodies today, persuasion works better than coercion, and
where rhetoric and moral authority, to say nothing of theological
expressiveness, do not do their work, people in parishes drag their
feet and fail to cooperate. In connectional bodies, members may
seem "disconnected" when they disagree with what the body advo-

cates. And congregationalist denominations—one thinks again of the Southern Baptist and Missouri Lutheran groups—may often sound more centralized and authoritative than many hierarchical denominations. But when it comes to the effect of social statements and political convictions, all groups tend to be on the same plane.

Another element that limits the effectiveness of religious bodies has to do with the fact that in a free republic, denominational leadership cannot impose legal penalties when coercion of its membership fails. It can only resort to continuing attempts at persuasion. Or such leadership must work with the expectation that there will at least be a stigma when fellow believers see a person disciplined for following political lines that diverge from church teaching.

For a concrete illustration, take the "seamless garment" in Roman Catholicism. Leaders like the late Cardinal Joseph Bernardin of Chicago attempted by persuasion to link all life issues, from abortion to capital punishment and physician-assisted suicide, into a common cause, a "seamless garment." Plenty of individuals in the church were antiabortion and self-described pro-life partisans, but they also favored capital punishment. Many spoke up for life in opposing the death penalty but did not link that advocacy to consistent support for fetal life. Bernardin worked with people who putatively shared a common commitment inside Catholicism but as individuals on various grounds differed in their choice of causes and commitments.

Catholicism makes some coercive claims on individuals, but these generally prove ineffective. The archbishop of San Diego in 1990 threatened to excommunicate a Catholic legislator if she kept supporting pro-choice causes and legislation. At one time, such a threat would have been terrifying and effective: denial of the sacraments would mean a hazard to the prospects for eternal salvation to the punished Catholics. But in a time of internal diversity in the church and of high degrees of individual choice within it, this legislator could find plenty of other leaders—theologians, if not bishops—who would back her, also on Catholic grounds. Her conscience would be clear and her political decisions free. Such a situation blunts efforts by her church to speak with one voice and to "throw its weight around" in legislative campaigns. But she will reason that Catholic consciences can be formed in a variety of ways, most of them capable of enhancing individual life and the health of the body politic.

One expects some sense of connection between the theological passion of a denomination and its social program. Some modern Methodists have observed that when John Wesley worked with a mere seventy thousand people in Britain and America, he seemed to have more influence than ten million United Methodists have today, when less passion goes into what Wesley would have called "spreading scriptural holiness throughout the land." Numbers and finances count, but they are not the only factors that spell political potency among denominations.

While church bodies have always shown the tendency to split— there were even papal schisms in the Middle Ages—and while schisms are still threats in denominations today when social issues like homosexuality come up, the main difference here between past and present has to do with the media, which shape believers' and members' minds and hearts. Accompanying the variety of choices portrayed in the media has been an increase in freedom. To be brought up, as many are, in the belief that "outside this church there is no salvation" or to fear ostracism for deviance, independence, or troublemaking in small town life is one thing. In cultures where people frequently move from place to place, there are many influences. They have great freedom to move on. Denominations are thus less likely to push their members too far. We could find illustrations of this in all denominations. Fear of the loss of members, as compromising as that sounds to the purist or absolutist, is itself part of the politics of denominations.

Thus leadership in many denominations might be ready to go much further in endorsing legislation that its opponents call "progay"; it has to back off when it fears that a schism would result from too forceful a resolution of debated issues.

Where the cost of abortions may be part of a denominations' medical policy program or where the denomination invests pension funds in controversial social programs, reaction from those who oppose these may be so strong that the religious bodies have to go back to the drawing board, to redraft policies, to buy time.

When the Presbyterians, through their agencies and bureaus, supported with denominational funds the cause of radical black activist Angela Davis, there was much grumbling. Some even expressed rage and withheld contributions when the collection plate was passed. Something similar occurred in the case of a famed Re-Imagining Conference, at which what looked to many like a secular feminist political agenda obscured classic Presbyterian understandings, and delegates knew that some denominational funds had been put to work at the conference. Again, the result was grumbling, rage, and a closing of pocketbooks. Though tensions may rise on the local level, politicians gradually learn how seriously to take denominational pronouncements. Their staffs learn to feed them information or write them speeches that reflect awareness of the power of various groups. A southern politician whose policies counter the very public views of the Southern Baptist Convention will be in a different position from one who pays no attention to them in a Catholic precinct in Boston. Going against Latter-day Saints policy in Utah is high-risk, whereas supporting the Equal Rights Amendment, which the Mormons at least in their own way opposed, was not "religiously" expensive in a liberal district in Manhattan.

Similarly, if the United Methodist Church passes dozens of resolutions in General Conference, the legislator will not be bluffed into overresponse if he or she is also a Methodist or has never met one who agrees with what a convention passed.

Financial Resources

The presence of denominational lobbies in Washington and sometimes in state capitals often goes unnoticed. The Southern Baptist Christian Life Commission and the United Methodist General

Board of Church and Society are typical. When the General Conference of the Methodists acts on issues every four years, the Methodists' lobby—headquartered only a couple of hundred yards from the Capitol—goes into action and represents the concerns. When the Baptists' commission takes a stand—for example, to oppose obscenity in movies or literature and to seek many kinds of legislation—its voice in Washington is expected to be heard. Of course, in many cases, a gap is evident between Washington and the local level. The political instincts of legislators come into play, and they have a way of sorting out voices with political clout from those without it. So to some extent the system works.

Diversity

Accommodating pluralism within the denomination can lead to filtered, well-considered stands. Yet even though politicians may be respectful of most religious leadership, for a variety of reasons—many of them born of genuine respect for religion in general and certain religions in particular—they also learn to do some discriminating when they get a denominational pronouncement. On one level, they may be quite astute in assessing the degree to which such a statement papers over the reality of internal diversity. On another level, a careful reading of such voted-on documents can reveal how diversity has flavored the stand. One can deduce from it something of the power of diversity in such units.

One cynical observer has said that "God walks strangely down the middle of the road" in most denominational public pronouncements. Some denominations may have become so identified with a political outlook or ideology that the middle disappears. Today's Southern Baptist Convention allows itself to take what many politicos think are extreme positions but seems to have the votes to back the viewpoint. The "peace churches" can take antiwar stands of a sort that under ordinary circumstances no one could sell to national bodies of other kinds of churches.

In most church bodies, however, committees, study groups, and task forces themselves are salted with people representing extremes who must ultimately formulate, with moderates, statements that can be sold to a voting body of the denomination. The politician can unearth what these more extreme views were and learn from the now suppressed or modified expressions of diversity.

Denominational diversity can also lead to slow decision making, result in watered-down positions to satisfy the diverse membership, and make the denominational voice politically impotent. Sometimes individuals who see themselves as wielding power boil matters down to the purely practical.

Listing denominations as agencies of power in politics does not do justice to the ways in which many members withhold consent from their church bodies. Some denominations that are on record as being pro-choice on abortion have thousands of presumably unhappy pro-life members. By no means did all Catholics go along with their bishops' statements on nuclear weaponry or the economy. Presbyterians have battled for a century over social and political issues and settled many of them only temporarily or with small majorities. The losing minorities ask, in what way is a bare majority the "voice of Presbyterianism"?

Or a person may be a member of a denomination but will get all her political signals from Focus on the Family or some other paradenominational movement. She may resent having her denomination speak up through convention vote and task force on an issue but will gladly sign up for and speak for a voluntary agency or interest group.

The gatekeeper between the national bodies and the local churches again tends to be priest, pastor, or rabbi. He or she can shield members from denominational pronouncements unless they are so bold and sensational that the press covers them and brings them to lay attention. The same cleric can at once gain pastoral credibility and help move people who might otherwise not see connections

between theology, religious life, and politics or may see it all differently than if they remain untutored, unconfronted, or left unaware
of denominational action. Still, no longer is it true that "what the
bishop says, goes." More often a pastor in a populist congregational
body, sometimes fundamentalist, has more power and is cited more
regularly in political contexts than any hierarch. And this is especially the case in today's emergent megachurches. They are often
gathered around credible and charismatic leaders whose views on
social and political themes are more readily adopted by their members than those of remote bishops or summertime conventions.

A Testing Ground for New Ideas

The denomination can also serve as a testing ground for church and
synagogue people who act outside their confines. For example, the
United Methodists in 1964 and 1968 prepared study documents in
the form of what they called the Family Life Statement. These documents defined the emergent family in some nontraditional ways
and included some mention of same-sex unions. The reaction to
these statements from individual and congregational sources gave
leadership some sense of how far to push parishioners as they voted
at national conventions. Spring something too suddenly on convention voters, they recognized, and they will provoke a backlash.
The denomination is more efficient than the ecumenical agency or
independent interest group for developing tentative statements and
getting them studied.

One special problem in the case of denominational involvement
has to do with the nature of bureaucratic and task force life. As-
semble a conference on, say, the family, and let people from many
denominations speak. Unless they are called to voice opinions based
on their creed, it will often turn out that some Lutherans, Episcopalians, and Catholics will sound more like each other than any of
them will sound like their fellow believers back home. The conference participants may be the advance guard, ahead of the membership. It is their professional duty to be alert to trends and research

in the areas of their expertise. Or the elite may be behind the regular constituency because the members are on front lines and denominational voices are sequestered in relatively safe headquarters.

Administrative and Financial Change

The political power of denominations has decreased because of administrative and financial change, primarily due to staff cuts and smaller administrative budgets in most denominations. A contributing factor is the power of the local in a world where people who are religious like to have some sense that they can make a difference. This means that they do not send funds so readily to headquarters.

Another factor is competitive parachurches and other voluntary associations. Organizations like Bread for the World or World Vision, no enemies of the denominations and agencies that trade off energies nurtured in the denominations and congregations, can focus more vividly and work more efficiently on their fronts than denominations, with their general programs, can.

Add to this the growing suspicion and cynicism of larger organizations in the world of religion. These can be and sometimes are remote and unresponsive.

Finally, social forces have diminished denominational power. Sociologists point out that the phenomenon of switching from one denomination to another is very common today. Many members change their affiliations, thanks in large part to mixed marriage. They lose all sense of loyalty to the religious body that once had commanded it. Yet the church bodies continue to have full agendas. Most denominations are "broke but busy." They have cut staffs in the face of declining revenues. Not that members are contributing less: religion still commands by far the largest share of charitable giving. But the trend is to focus on the local scene, where institutional expenses have grown and where financial strategies can be more firmly controlled than at headquarters. The result is that for merely practical reasons, denominations have lost some political power, because it was often from the financially starved headquarters that political statements and efforts emerged.

Summary

Given the anti-institutional view of many Americans in recent decades and their suspicion of the religious establishment, along with drastic social changes, the denomination, invented in the eighteenth century, is sometimes seen as fading and moving toward death at the beginning of the twenty-first. Studebaker cars, Underwood typewriters, and silent movies had their day and then were displaced; nothing lasts forever. So the denomination may be waning, and its political potential with it. The act of opening a phone book and finding "Vineyard Christian Fellowship," "Love Center Full Gospel Church," "Over the Mountain Christian Church," or "Because He Lives"—as listed in the Birmingham, Alabama, phone book—may well lead one to call into question the meaning and power of Methodism or Mormonism. At the very least, the denominational monopoly is gone.

If denominations are fading, one must also note that during their decline and fall, many are fighting over the facades and relics. Each summer, in the church convention season, the media pay attention to the denominations as they deal with mainly two issues, sex and authority, which add up to "dealing with controversy but staying together." When there are winners and losers and when minorities are made to feel unwelcome or be banished, as in the Southern Baptist and Missouri Lutheran battles, the winners command the spoils. They can act as if the benefits of victory are huge—large enough to contribute to the political power of those church bodies and give them license to act as if with a single voice.

Denominations that would speak politically face challenge also from ecumenical forces, which often create the impression that great numbers of voters support their task forces and commissions. Add this understanding of pressure from above, as it were, to the starvation from below, in the congregations; from alongside, in the parachurch agencies; and by the new, the nondenominational megachurch movements, and it becomes ever more clear that denominationalism is waning in our time.

However, denominations are not likely to disappear. They occupy a certain niche in the organization of American religion and among the ways individuals and congregations reach out beyond the local. They often share confessions of faith and agree on denominational rites and outlooks. It is quite natural for most of them to see their faith put to work corporately, so the denomination had become a premier way of going about this. It helps provide citizens with paths through the mazes of religious pluralism and relativism. The denomination may no longer be regarded as the sole custodian of the sole truth. The church body as a marker of boundaries around doctrine and practice has yielded to other kinds of grouping. Yet coherences do remain, and there are efforts within denominations of many sorts to evoke and even coerce assent to doctrines and applications. Thus when in 1998 the Southern Baptist Convention voted that the biblical injunction for wives "to submit" to their husbands must rule the home today, the voters at the summer convention implied that one could not be a good Baptist and yet ignore the vote, full of political implications as it is.

Some political figures are ready to say they regret the dissipation of denominational voices and energies. They would welcome stronger denominational expressions on the public, social, and political fronts. Why? For one thing, such voices counter the individualism that makes it harder for religious voices to be heard. They represent more believers' interests than the more narrowly focused activist groups do. Denominations provide locales for the confronting of scriptures and traditions in the context of whole ministries, whereas interest groups represent only small and often unrepresentative parts of these. When denominational groups, as in Reform and Conservative Judaism, speak with clear and relatively united voices, as they did in the early years of Israel's existence, they demonstrably do have influence. And the spiritual witness of the denominations may convey the bearing of some kinds of truth not often heard in the political arena, with all its compromise.

The denomination shares in what sociologist Mark Chaves has chronicled as a crisis of authority that afflicts leaders at their relative remove more than it hits local pastors.[4] It is uncertain in every case as to how much authority was given to denominational electees to office or professional agents or voluntary spokespersons. It is difficult for publics to discern how to relate to the various voices that speak in the name of a particular denomination of which they do not seem to be representative. Despite this trend, the voice of denominational task forces, leaders, researchers, and attendees at national and ecumenical conventions remains a key, if not any longer the key, to interpreting texts, loyalties, and power in American public religion.

Although the limits of denominational power are apparent, there are at least some instances in which, especially if accompanied by parachurch interest groups and agencies, they still have or may regain some direct influence. How church bodies prepare individual hearts and minds through sermons, policy statements, disseminated research, and task forces or commissions can have indirect bearing when members as voters or members as interest-group participants intervene in the voting processes.

Denominations, as they involve themselves with political issues from abortion to euthanasia, school prayer, and war and peace were once protective and dismissed as sectarian. Today it is on the social issues and political front that they have their greatest ecumenical consequence. They form alliances with counterparts in other denominations who share their views. They might do well to be more aware of the pros and cons of such a trend, assuming that they have positive views of the effects of ecumenical agencies.

Ecumenical Agencies

It goes almost without saying that members of individual congregations stand a good chance of being able to be heard in respect to the political stances and governmental involvements of these local bodies. Most Protestant churches have only a few hundred members, and only several scores of them would take active roles shaping policy. There are good chances for face-to-face relations and personal entanglements. Mention government or politics to your congregation, and you will hear a wide range of responses—most of them informed.

For that same smaller majority of citizens and believers who are active in the organized and institutional life of churches, synagogues, and other such agencies, it is natural to assume that many will care about denominational life. Denominations may not be what they used to be, but they do perform many useful functions. If you are a Presbyterian and the General Assembly makes a pronouncement on politics and you find out about it, you will find yourself automatically taking some sort of stand on the issue: "How dare those delegates say that Presbyterians are for boycotting lettuce in order to help the farmworkers?" or "Hooray! Our church is showing its conscience and identifying with oppressed people." If you are a Catholic committed to an unmonitored free market and the bishops write a letter on the economy that looks like welfare statism, you will be made highly aware of it and will be engaged. If you are a pro-choice Catholic and the bishops say that antiabortion approaches are the only licit ones, you will be greatly aware of their proclamations and will seek to be disengaged.

The Role of Interchurch Organizations

When we come to the interchurch or interreligious organization, one of the twentieth century's most vital and enterprising forms of advancing religious engagement with the political order, a different picture emerges. So much of what the local, state, national, and world councils of churches and federations of religions talk about and do seems remote. Individuals do not "join" such councils of churches; their church bodies do. If one has little say in the political pronouncements or governmental involvements of one's denomination, it is sure that the ecumenical or interchurch organization will

be doubly insulated from the members and twice as hard to moni-
tor or affect.

Much of this interchurch and interreligious activity is of a top-
down nature. Popes and bishops, presidents and moderators, task
forces and commissions make studies and formulate position papers
about which individual church members learn at third hand. During the century in which ecumenical and interchurch connections
became ever more feasible and favored, believers paradoxically
began to put new emphasis on the local. Influenced, of course, by
mass media and aware of the power of corporations and other large
forces, believers still chose to favor institutions where they could
make a difference. Ecumenical organizations were not that accessible to most of them.

A story from our own experience may illuminate this point. In
1960, at the Faith and Order Commission of the World Council of
Churches (WCC), the leaders were attempting to draft an answer
to the question "What is the nature of the unity we seek?" They
spoke eloquently of the fact that all who were in Christ should
"come to a fully committed fellowship." How astonished we were
to see that the translators and typists from Geneva, WCC headquarters, had rendered this as "a full committee fellowship"! What
they had failed to reason out was that what councils did through
committees, bureaucracies, and task forces had little to do with
the commitment of the faithful in their various communities.

Having said all that, however, it is still important to identify the
kinds of power the interchurch and interreligious agencies do have.
Opponents did what they could to magnify the power of the councils by sending around materials that the disseminators presumed
would be offensive to the locals in an effort to get them to withhold
support or even leave the councils. WCC leaders and gatherings for
some of the Cold War and postcolonial decades excoriated the
United States and affluent Western European nations for being in-
sensitive, even for dominating the poor world. To the American
right, the WCC looked soft on communism. The council's enemies

certainly knew that it had some sort of power. And of course, it was involved in human rights struggles and relief programs that had bearings on government—and won favor from many who applauded this. So we shall examine the current state of such ecumenical agencies as instruments for political and governmental thought and action.

Around the middle of the twentieth century, farseeing people anticipated the dwindling of other religious agencies of power in the face of fledgling ecumenical and interfaith movements. People of various faiths had seen the limits of individual, congregational, and denominational action. Over the course of time, Jewish, Muslim, and non-Western religious representatives became active in interfaith groups that began to assert themselves politically, but most of the transdenominational action groups were Christian. After the Vatican Council ended in 1962, these could be Protestant- and Catholic-linked. For most of the century, however, Protestants, sometimes mixed with Eastern Orthodox Christians, dominated the ecumenical scene and tried to deliver "divisions" or votes in the political arena.

The History of Ecumenism

Since not all citizens, including all religious citizens, are at home with the vocabulary of ecumenism and the story of its rise, we should spend a minute reviewing both.

Christians had divided between East and West in the eleventh century and, in the West, between Protestant and Catholic in the sixteenth. Ever after, Protestants split, innovated, traveled, and in the process invented a quilt or mosaic of thousands of separate and often competitive bodies.

The ecumenical movement was inspired by the vision of missionaries, laypeople, students, and cosmopolites, who with a heady spirit and progressive theology began to report about the frustration of their work because Christian missionaries were dividing their spoils abroad. Meanwhile Christian people of action found their voices muffled and their efforts blunted because they spoke up separately. They had no common strategy. They were small and weak. They did not use all the resources they could have had they been linked. They undercut each other or acted in ignorance of what others could do.

Historians usually describe an International Missionary Conference in Edinburgh, Scotland, in 1910 as the scene of the formal birth of the new movement they called "ecumenical," using a Greek-based word that referred to the whole inhabited world. Two years before that, the churches that later came to be called mainstream Protestant participated in founding the Federal Council of Churches. In 1950, it was replaced by the National Council of the Churches of Christ in the USA (NCC). After two world wars that occurred mainly on "Christian" soil, and thanks to the patient endeavors of leaders in movements such as Faith and Order and Life and Work, the ecumenical flicker ignited at the 1948 formation of the World Council of Churches (WCC).

Doings in Amsterdam, where that council was born, or Geneva, where it was headquartered, may seem remote from American politics or American governing. But the WCC has a domestic office in New York, and it aspires to speak for non–Roman Catholic Christians of many sorts around the world. It had become clear that many of the issues with which religious groups were poised to deal were international and have intranational bearing. As noted, when the WCC leadership spoke out during the Cold War, its words were repeated incessantly by its enemies, to the point that congregants of nonmember churches and adherents who disagreed with much of the council's expression no doubt knew more about the WCC than those who mildly favored it. Here are a few illustrations:

> No sooner had the National Council of Churches formed in 1950 than the National Lay Committee, made up of people within the constituent denominations, organized to oppose its immediate policy declarations. Most of the Lay Committee represented business interests and

were offended by what they saw as liberal, sometimes socialist, tendencies in council leadership.

———

This was the McCarthy era, when Senator Joseph Mc-
Carthy and the House Un-American Activities Committee suspected the American leadership in the World
Council of Churches of being too soft on communism.
The council included Russian Orthodox and other
churches from behind the Iron Curtain, and Western ecumenical leaders were staying in touch with them and
often spoke uncritically of them. When the council
drafted its "Basic Christian Principles and Assumptions
for Economic Life," the Lay Committee voted 47 to 0
against it as "socialist." Stick to religion, not politics, was
the word from the economic conservatives.

———

The National Council of Churches provided the most
consistent Protestant leadership in the civil rights struggles of the 1950s and 1960s, working side by side with
Catholic and Jewish integrationist forces. In the constituent denominations, especially in the South, there
were strong resistant and segregationist elements, and
they targeted the NCC for opposition.

———

During the Vietnam War, even before the American majority opposed it, the NCC dissented against American
military policy—again joining ranks with Catholic and
Jewish leaders. The opposition forces, often described as
"hawks" or "the right," spoke up vehemently and sometimes worked to have funding withheld from ecumenical

organizations. While many members of constituent denominations may have paid little attention to such organizations, surrounded as these were by so many
dissenters, enemies of the NCC gave considerable pub-
licity to council words that looked subversive. In 1966,
the NCC in assembly questioned "whether U.S.A. policy does not rely too heavily upon a massive military intervention."[5] But it was not ready to call for instant
withdrawal of forces. By 1969, however, the council addressed the Nixon administration with a call for a coalition government including Vietnamese communists—an
outrage to opponents of such a policy and thus of the
council. Carl Henry, editor of *Christianity Today,* an
evangelical magazine, declared that the NCC had
moved beyond its competence.[6] And Paul Ramsey, a
noted Methodist theologian of moderate tendencies,
criticized the leaders again for lack of expertise.[7]

The World Council of Churches leadership backed Latin
American liberation theology, which drew on both biblical and Marxist sources—another offense to conservative Catholics and to Protestants on the political right.

William Howard, president of the NCC, visited "political prisoners" in American prisons—again, an act opposed by many in the constituent churches, who claimed
that there were no such prisoners.

In 1978, the WCC Committee on Justice and Service,
chaired by an American Baptist, approved a generous financial grant for humanitarian purposes to guerrilla

forces in Rhodesia (Zimbabwe). The committee had no
means of knowing whether the funds would go into arms
and thus left itself vulnerable to criticism.

———————

At World Council conclaves every six years, the American leadership tended to assent to criticisms by church
people from Eastern Europe and from the poor world
that Western European and American churches and nations were "imperialist," statements that made the WCC
seem out of step with the membership majorities in congregations and denominations.

Councils or federations did not exhaust the ecumenical or interfaith options. Some ecumenists envisioned an eventually re-
united Christendom, or at least Protestant-and-Orthodoxdom, a
"coming great church" that would by its unity fulfill the commands
and live into the promises of unity preserved in the New Testament.
If there was "one Lord, one baptism, one faith," as Paul wrote and
as all Christians believed and professed, should it not take concrete
and thus visible form in merged church bodies? Americans often
raised these questions and dreamed these dreams because in the eyes
of church unity folk, the church was more visibly divided in America than almost anywhere else.

Merger was hard to come by, however. Despite great efforts at
unity in the early and mid-twentieth century, counterforces were
strong. Members of most churches did not want to give up their distinctive characteristics or take on those of others, as they might or
must in a full merger. For every person who spoke up for homoge-
nizing, blending, and cooperative efforts, there was someone who
saw Christian—and political—potential in heterogeneous, particular, and competitive efforts. If Christian unity was supposed to advance conversion of unreached people and make the church more
attractive, why, some asked, did most evangelizing efforts appear

among non- and even antiecumenical elements? Who wanted to give up the patterns of worship and hymnody or the special practices of their own church?

In the United States, there were few mergers across denominational and ethnic lines. The 1957 formation of the United Church of Christ in the United States was a rare exception. Most mergers occurred between separate kin in Presbyterian, Methodist, Lutheran, and other bodies.

Many of these separated bodies—Presbyterian and Methodist in particular—had divided on regional lines before the Civil War. Lutherans were divided because they came as immigrants from numerous European nations and styles of church life or had engaged in doctrinal disputes. Now they put their houses in order. This in itself was a difficult task, but not as adventuresome as denominational mergings across family lines—for example, merging Methodist and Baptist—would have been.

More satisfying was the pattern in which churches kept their identity and autonomy but worked through formal councils or federations. This conciliar pattern was attractive because it permitted compromise and coalitions that encouraged common expression, including of political sorts, without hazard to what communions held separately. Leaders of councils, be they global, national, regional, statewide, or local, had to make it clear that cooperating churches did not surrender autonomy and that not everyone in the member churches or the churches themselves had to agree with everything that went on in state or national councils. Here was Christian unity well combined with Christian freedom.

So successful were the councils and federations of mainstream and liberal Protestants that they found mirror images in similar agencies among the more conservative "antiecumenical" denominations. In 1941, fundamentalists organized the American Council of Christian Churches, and a year later, the much more effective National Association of Evangelicals (NAE) was formed. The NAE has been careful not to be too explicit about its political interests, since it cannot always speak for all the denominations in it, but there is no doubt that its words have been heard in high councils of government. For example, protecting the interests of religious broadcasters, though the conservatives among them have their own National Association of Religious Broadcasters, involves political participation.

In this context of enlargement beyond mainstream Protestant ecumenism, the interfaith movement deserves notice. Prime among its agencies is the National Conference for Community and Justice (NCCJ). It has no member churches, only members. Yet it has gained credibility as the voice of cooperators beyond the bounds of Christianity. Concerned as it is with issues of church and state, it is practically by definition involved with politics. Taken with the Christian ecumenical fronts, the NCCJ and its kin further demonstrate that this has been a century of convergences toward cooperation on the public front and the political scene.

Problems

It is apparent that the very features that made councils of autonomous churches attractive also limited them politically. Let us examine a few of these limitations.

Generals Without Armies

To return to the images behind this chapter: the ecumenical "army" was too divided to have many effective "divisions." Enemies of the councils called the leaders "generals without armies." The ecumenical front could not deliver votes; individuals enjoyed their own individual autonomy and their congregational and denominational agencies and used these as filters and shields to prevent them from being represented or spoken for.

Jeopardizing Integrity

We have spoken of enemies and critics of ecumenical and interfaith agencies. Some of these ground their criticism in theological issues that need not concern us here as much as their political actions and statements. Critics contend that even in movements toward unity where each element is assured of autonomy, compromises must be made that jeopardize integrity. One advocate of the National Association of Evangelicals, when it came on the scene to contend against the National Council of Churches, called his book *Cooperation Without Compromise*, his slap at what he regarded as sellouts of theology in the mainstream ecumenical groups.[8]

The author, James DeForest Murch, contended in language familiar in that day but less so now that "evangelicals do not want the Church in politics." As for the church councils, "Never was cooperation with compromise more charmingly sought." The councils were liberal, and liberalism was "the great apostasy." The evangelicals had to oppose the ecumenical councils and federations in what had been turning out to be "the battle of the century." The World Council was cooperating with an impending "world socialism and world dictatorship." Thus "the growing interest of Moscow in the use of the World Council of Churches, the National Council of Churches (USA) and UNESCO to further Communist aims needs to be watched eagerly."[9]

Mode of Operation

The most constant criticism, however, had less to do with the political stance than with the mode of operation of the councils. Thus the National Council in its early years and in its mid-twentieth-century prime liked to say that it spoke for tens of millions of Protestants. Methodist theologian Paul Ramsey's critique *Who Speaks for the Churches?* came to be a rallying point for critics from within. When enemies of the NCC would inform member churches of a particular council pronouncement, such members would react, Yes, who does speak for us? Who counted us in? We are unconsulted members of an unconsulted denomination. No opinion polls were taken. Some of the arguments in the pronouncements, critics argued, were based on readings of scripture that conflicted with those held by denominations or individuals—or were not based on scripture or traditional elements at all.

Concurrently, when suspicion developed against large institutions, the apparently larger ones like the National Council got written off as behemoths of big-time bureaucracy—even though the NCC's budget was not nearly as large as that of its vigorous opponent, the Southern Baptist Convention. Critics perceived the ecumenical agency to be more powerful than it truly was. Those who needed a bogey, a foil, a red flag to be used to rally their own troops found the local, state, and national churches satisfying such roles.

The process of determining who speaks and how looked subversive and unfair to many members. In their eyes, with some justification, they positioned people of certain theological and political stands to their left. Such perceptions were costly for the National Council and other ecumenical agencies. The harmful charge is that an elite of inbred, interactive spokespersons has commandeered the ecumenical pulpits, platforms, and press. They are responsive to each other, but not to their sponsoring bodies. The process they were to prepare for advocacy depends on research, study groups, and task forces, who prepare policy statements to be backed up by votes of central committees or a delegate or two out of a church body of five million unconsulted and often uninformed people. Along the way, the voice of the dissenter does not get heard.

Limited Finances

Another limitation of councils is related to finances. Characteristically, the ecumenical groups to which denominations are committed are the last to be added and the first to be dropped when denominations set budgets. The leaders know that funds stay close to home, in the various synods or other jurisdictions—each of which has trouble collecting these funds from congregations and resists sending it all in to headquarters, as local missions and hence expenses grow.

Without adequate funding, of course, interfaith agencies cannot be as productive as their promise suggests. The politician who sees the energies that the winners in Southern Baptist denominational conflicts invest in church-state issues is likely to run into agitated members of their convention. Much rarer is the officeholder who is aware of the underbudgeted, understaffed state or national council.

Benefits

But despite their problems, the councils offer a number of benefits to their members.

Voice for the Voiceless

Who, then, listens to the councils? Leaders admit that few people do, but there are selective exceptions. The National Council of Churches and the Catholic Bishops' Councils were widely quoted in opposition to Operation Desert Storm—even though the Bush administration in the end ignored their positions. These councils are often considered the voices of the otherwise voiceless. They can generate policies for debate in denominations that might otherwise have neglected them. Their teaching roles remain stronger than their vote-getting or vote-blocking powers. They often bring to mind the voice of the world church where the local parish may be too provincial or insular to cause others to reckon with it. Sometimes the councils pull denominations into more expansive positions, as when four decades ago, the National Council of Churches helped draw the United Methodists of Texas into more open stands on racial issues.

Media Manipulation

In some respects, the councils have found more power through media news coverage than through gathered constituencies. They are often present on the metropolitan scene, more ready with responses to issues than the denominations, with their biennial or quadrennial meetings and relative silence in between, or the local congregations.

Yet to understand the character of contemporary ecumenical expression, it is wise to pay attention to the ad hoc and sometimes single-issue constituencies that draw people across denominational boundaries and out of congregations. We will discuss them at length in Chapter Five, for they seem to have become the most potent religious forms when social, economic, political, and public issues crowd the agendas.

Public Involvement

To focus as closely as we have on the limitations of ecumenical and interfaith potential and action is to distort the record. The enterprise of interchurch and interfaith relations has amounted to much more than generals without armies, spokespersons without hearers, and bureaucracies without followings. The record of public involvement thanks to councils, federations, and associations is extensive. Some of the religious bodies' activities were inspired by governmental needs and contacts.

We may have overstressed the National and World Councils of Churches at the expense of various interdenominational Jewish organizations or the National Association of Evangelicals. The former were on the scene constantly where the interests of Israel were involved, and the State Department made few moves in the Middle East without at least becoming aware of what synagogue-goers thought. The National Association of Evangelicals, formed in 1942, increasingly positioned itself to work with government, especially during Republican presidencies, just as the National Council was more in favor during the Democratic Kennedy and Johnson administrations. Not only did the ecumenical groups support relief efforts and foreign aid that was helpful to the U.S. government, but they also found a ready ear among legislators on issues that concerned them. Most recently, religious groups have been consulted on such issues as universal health care and physician-assisted suicide.

Councils of churches and ecumenical or interfaith agencies have been involved in war relief and immigration activities, most of which involve political negotiation. They advance voluntary groups, many of which put tax funds to work alongside funds gained from the voluntary religious sector. Councils and interfaith groups have often been on the political front lines in defense of the free exercise of religion on the part of even the smallest, most exotic, and most despised of religious groups. When the U.S. Senate investigated the Unification Church or when the Southern Baptist Convention claimed that it was being infringed on with respect to workplace policies, many denominational leaders "climbed Capitol Hill" to make their voices heard. They found that councils and associations made mobilization easier and more effective than it would have been with denominations only.

Ecumenical forces are powers with which to reckon and voices that want to be heard. The parachurches to which we shall turn attention in Chapter Five have taken on some of their roles in recent decades, further crowding and drawing attention from the ecumenical councils and federations. Yet they survive, active and speaking out. But they no longer have the field to themselves and keep picking up new and efficient rivals.

Ecumenical agencies have been slighted as interest groups crowd in on them. During the 1996 presidential campaign, the Republican candidates for president and vice president were scheduled to meet with the National Council of Churches but canceled on rather casual grounds—something they would not have done if the date had been with, say, the Christian Coalition. Assuming that these Republicans were relatively astute politicians, their advisers and their own observations must have convinced them that there were not many votes to be won or lost on the NAE front. The National Council of Churches, for all its long history of political intervention, has sometimes been a quiet player in presidential campaigns during the past quarter century and sometimes not a player at all.

Though Internal Revenue Service policies and membership interests may have kept the leadership from formal endorsement of candidates, it is obvious that the more liberal NCC was more inclined to back Democratic contenders, and the NAE, also constrained from formal endorsements, cheered and worked for Republican presidents Nixon and Reagan.

Religious Institutions and Contemporary Political Activity

All through the nineteenth century, visionary and practical people alike welcomed congregational life but disdained denominational competition and practices of mutual exclusion. They invented new forms with practical and sometimes theological interaction, but until the twentieth century, few of these would be classified as ecumenical. In every case, they became what French visitor Alexis de Tocqueville called them in the 1830s: associations. "Americans of all ages, all stations of life, and all types of disposition are forever forming associations," Tocqueville wrote. "They are not only commercial and industrial associations in which all take part, but others of a thousand different types—religious, moral, serious, futile, very general and very limited, immensely large and very minute."[10] These associations, the Frenchman thought, were the heart of creative life in the democracy he observed and congratulated. Through them, people would pool their separate interests to make a difference in the world—for themselves, their fellow believers, and the larger culture.

Some historians note that these groups have prospered in a competitive religious marketplace. Sometimes groups have dreamed up and peddled their spiritual products, advertising them well and winning converts by outdoing others with weaker products. Or religious groups have tested the market, assessing people's hungers and then directing their efforts toward satisfying those needs. Protestant denominations were pioneers in this religious competition after the Revolution, but others have followed their model. Even in Catholicism, where the boundaries of parishes are set by bishops, parishioners shop among possibilities in search of the most congenial congregations. Similarly, Jews are free to join Orthodox, Conservative, Reform, or Reconstruction congregations depending on their personal preferences, which places the different branches in competition with one another for adherents.

So while congregations, denominations, and ecumenical agencies are officially disestablished—freestanding in respect to government—and hence not directly involved in the political orbit, traditional religious institutions inevitably come into all kinds of contact with politics and government. Sociologist Henri Desroche has observed three main ways religious adherents relate to the world around them. In most cases, Desroche argues, religious people attest to the doings of the government with its popular majority. They support it, give it sacred sanction, and promote civil authorities that are congenial and generous to them. In a minority of cases, they contest. While sharing the basic assumptions of the larger society, they nevertheless criticize it with an intent to purify it. And a still smaller minority—sometimes even a minority of one—protests. That is, they see themselves serving the public by denouncing the ways of the larger society virtually en masse and then calling down divine sanction for their own prophesying against the political and moral order then in favor.[11]

To the degree that congregations, denominations, and agencies attest, contest, or protest, they become involved in politics. They may do this only to the point of lobbying for better zoning laws and against noisemaking around their sacred edifice. More of them do move somewhat further into the political waters, and many are explicit about their commitments. In various guises, then, congregations, denominations, and associations have inevitably played key roles in public life, often explicitly in politics.

The Wall of Separation

At this point, one might ask what has happened to the wall of separation between church and state. Doesn't this cherished American notion exclude congregations, denominations, and ecumenical agencies from direct involvement in politics? Recall that the "wall of separation" metaphor cannot be found in the United States Constitution or the Bill of Rights; it comes from a letter President Thomas Jefferson sent to Connecticut's Danbury Baptist Association in 1802. Once dismissed by Chief Justice William Rehnquist as merely a "short note of courtesy,"[12] Jefferson's letter nevertheless provided us with a metaphor that has come to dominate twentieth-century discussions of religion and politics.

Aside from a ban on religious tests for public office, the Constitution takes up the relationship between church and state only in the First Amendment. The language itself is limited and sparse: "Congress shall make no law respecting an establishment of religion or prohibiting the free exercise thereof." In those sixteen words, the founders spoke only of how the national government should relate to religion. Supporters of the new constitutional order knew better than to antagonize the states by saying anything about the proper relationship between state governments and religions, so the First Amendment addressed national concerns alone. When the Constitution and Bill of Rights were ratified, several states still supported legal church establishments. The favored religious group received governmental support the way public schools do today: all citizens paid for it, regardless of their attitude toward it or whether they made use of the institution. Dissent might be tolerated and exemptions from paying taxes for some of these dissenting religious groups might sometimes be granted, but churches remained established in most of the thirteen former colonies.

Those establishments slowly disappeared (the last by 1833), but it was not until the 1940s that the U.S. Supreme Court began to extend the First Amendment language to the states. The Court "incorporated" the Bill of Rights, making it apply to all the states, using language in the Fourteenth Amendment (a Reconstruction Era amendment designed to ensure the civil liberties of recently freed slaves). It was a controversial interpretation by the Court, and critics continue to challenge the legitimacy of applying the Bill of

Rights to the states. But after more than a half century of Supreme Court decisions, it seems likely that the Bill of Rights will continue to be binding on the states for the foreseeable future. Hence the First Amendment's strictures and assurances concerning religion now apply to all parts of American life.

But even applying the Bill of Rights to the states has not created a high and impregnable wall of separation between religion and government. Founder James Madison offers a more accurate characterization: there is a "line of distinction" between civil and religious authorities—a line that is often permeable, sometimes blurred, always contested.[13] In contemporary American life, church and state unavoidably and closely interact in many ways. To take the largest and most dramatic illustration, religious organizations through more than two centuries have enjoyed an exemption from paying property taxes. This policy undoubtedly costs municipalities all kinds of money, as valuable property generates no tax revenues, and all municipal citizens indirectly support religious organizations by virtue of the property taxes they pay for community services. Citizens even subsidize community services, such as police and fire protection, for religious groups.

One area that illustrates conflicts between church and state involves civil declarations of landmark status. For example, a congregation must enlarge its building to serve its worship needs, but the civil authority forbids any exterior alteration to the existing structure on legal landmark grounds.

Freedom for Religion, Freedom for Nonreligion

If individuals use religion to persuade, witness to, or inspire others, what happens to atheists, agnostics, and secularists? Though a distinct and mostly unorganized cultural minority, the nonreligious in America are equally concerned with public policy and the common good. Does the Constitution also guarantee them freedom of thought and action?

In the American circumstance, freedom of religion necessarily entails freedom for no religion at all. People who complain that secularists are already too much in the government's favor must remember that to the nonreligious, the culture is strongly biased in favor of religion as a motivator of individuals in the political order. Freedom for both sides best guarantees freedom for all.

One of the best protections against one ideology—whether religious or secular—coming to dominate society is the wide, and even wild, pluralism of American culture. In regions where one faith predominates (for example, in the Baptist South or in Mormon Utah), dissenting individuals—especially nonbelievers—may struggle to be heard. But the more that various groups speak up, the smaller the risk that one collective voice will monopolize public debate.

5

The Flourishing of Religious
Special-Interest Groups

*Thesis: For the foreseeable future, religious people
will funnel their political energies into interest groups
and voluntary associations.*

Special-interest groups, caucuses, movements, and causes—all of
them voluntary associations—have a long, controversial, and
still honored place in American politics. Prohibition would not
likely have become the law of the land had it not been for the
Women's Christian Temperance Union and the Anti-Saloon
League, organizations that date from 1874 and 1895, respectively.
These groups helped convince Congress to draft a constitutional
amendment and then to mobilize voters in the requisite number of
states for ratification. They were again prime agencies arguing
against repeal of Prohibition during the 1920s.

In more recent times, the Christian Legal Society and a number
of other legal organizations helped advance church-state causes to
the U.S. Supreme Court. Their alertness and persistence have undoubtedly shaped Court rulings in a number of cases. Americans
United, originally Protestants and Other Americans United for Separation of Church and State, similarly worked the church-state
front, often in efforts to portray Catholics as seekers of privilege for
their church. Various creationist organizations were successful in

getting the Arkansas and Alabama state legislatures to pass laws curtailing the teaching of evolution in the public schools.

In the civil rights campaign, the Southern Christian Leadership Conference was a prime mobilizer, using explicitly religious motives to organize and agitate; the American Black Baptist Caucus is one of many successors. Indeed, African American, Jewish, Catholic, and mainstream Protestant special-purpose groups have long histories in the United States. In the last quarter of the twentieth century, evangelicals were the most effective at organizing voluntary groups engaged in lobbying, vote gathering, and policy formation. Focus on the Family and Concerned Women for America have been able to mobilize votes in Congress in support of conservative evangelical views on the family and women's roles.

How Interest Groups Form

Interest groups can form in at least two ways. In one, leaders initiate. They succeed in applying names to previously confusing realities. They draw lines between "us" and "them." They discuss the positive religious value of following this or that policy and the negative value of failing to do so. In effect, they create a problem or a vision of a problem for which they already have an answer.

The other way is for people to see a problem and to discern inadequacies in governmental and denominational approaches to it. They then begin to find ways to address it. They solicit the support of others and define themselves over against those who do not share the cause. They form or join a group.

The Religious Origins of Special-Purpose Groups

Princeton sociologist Robert Wuthnow regards special-purpose groups as an American tradition and has written about the ways in which they now rival denominations in political causes. In societies where there was a religious establishment or a monopoly by one group, all the "special purposes" were accomplished under the aegis of that establishment. Yet even so, people who discern new needs or have new proposals organize in particular ways. The Roman Catholic religious orders that specialize in nursing, education, or missions are examples of these. On Protestant soil, there were orders of deaconesses, "inner missions," relief agencies, and similar groups. In nations governed by, say, Shi'ite Muslims, the government may control most of the agencies, but there is still room for some special-purpose groups.

The Special Case of the United States

In the young United States, however, these groups found a hospitable climate for spawning ever more. Some historians point to the irony in the name of the Industrial Revolution, noting that few guns were fired and no treaties were signed. They observe that it was more a process than anything else. But other historians argue that the great explosion in invention, industrialization, and economic growth set off in the process qualifies as a full-fledged revolution.

The rise of voluntary associations and societies in the young republic of the United States was part of a similar creative explosion. In the early years of the nineteenth century, the weak federal government was neither empowered nor motivated to engage in welfare work. Church establishments were fading or already gone. At the same time, there was a continent to fill, a world for an eager first generation of foreign missionaries to win for Christ, and a myriad of social problems and needs for welfare and education. Spontaneously, across the former colonies and in all the churches, laypeople and some professionals began forming associations of the sort that impressed Alexis de Tocqueville so much on his visit to the United States in the 1830s.

Some associations were directly political. They organized to help pass legislation—against dueling, for instance, or prohibiting mail delivery on Sunday. Some tried to shift from the promotion of temperance to calling for the outright prohibition of liquor, a move that necessitated political organizing and agitation. Abolition, a cause often associated with religion, could not be accomplished without legislation, which meant politics or, in its breakdown, war. The nineteenth-century register of religious associations with political goals is extensive.

As non-Protestant immigrants arrived in great numbers late in the century, they soon learned to follow the pattern and protect themselves or promote their causes through associations. Catholic groups such as the Knights of Columbus flourished and had political effects. From the beginning, Jews formed relief societies and put great energies into them in the twentieth century. Some of these were directly political. The birth of Israel in 1948, for example, demonstrated the increasing persuasiveness of Jewish special-purpose groups in national politics.

But it was liberal Protestants who had a head start in developing associations and agencies to support the legislative programs connected with various social gospels and social Christianity. By the middle of the twentieth century—especially after the New Deal in 1933 began to draw ever more energy to the federal government—the religious groups found it necessary to create agencies through which they could continue to serve and to agitate for legislative change.

The Growing Importance and Effectiveness of Voluntary Religious Associations

Given the long history of voluntary religious associations in politics, why do they appear to be so important and effective now? Among the answers to that question would be factors such as these:

- They are the survivors; as denominations and ecumenical agencies lost some of their power, these voluntary groups gained comparatively and filled a vacuum.

- Modern communications—broadcasting, rapid mail, the Internet—have made it easier than before for agencies with relatively low budgets to attract national constituencies, inform them, and mobilize them.

- Ever since the New Deal in 1933, when the government took over many social service functions that had been the virtual monopoly of religious groups, and through the 1950s and 1960s, when the implications of life in a welfare state became ever more clear, the religious groups learned that they had to intervene in governmental work and policy if they wanted to continue to have access to publics they could serve.

- The last four decades of the twentieth century were times of great upheaval—the civil rights movement, welfare policies, the Vietnam War, culture wars, and the like—and in such times, the voice of the individual can be lost, and the voice of traditional institutions of religion are often tardy, compromised, or compromising, as special-interest groups do not have to be.

- New voices have begun to be heard, particularly African American voices in the cities and evangelical activists nationally. They have learned from the mistakes of others. They have learned to gather the like-minded so they can speak clearly. They have negative views of secular cultural drift and liberal adaptation to it. They have mobilized with great resources and imagination.

- The "federalization of life" has disturbed conservatives, who have less difficulty influencing the local scene, where "our kind" may predominate, than making an impact in the welter of pluralism; this change has been particularly influenced by the Supreme Court and its decisions.

- Conservatives were capable of summoning people of considerable talent, energy, focus, and drive to provide leadership. Many of the moderates and liberals were so eager to work with people who did not share their particular religious outlook that they did not do well at summoning support, finding proper accents and goals, and working out strategies.

For a variety of reasons, some of which we will note in our discussion, the conservatives became the most visible religious workers on the political scene. They reacted and formed new associations or rehabilitated old ones. Whenever these came to be perceived as threatening to others or perhaps too effective on their own, editorialists of secular bent evoked the "separation of church and state" and urged that the conservatives be held back or even suppressed by law for mixing religion and regime. Unfair! responded the newly organized conservatives, who pointed out that the same editorialists had not customarily criticized the Southern Christian Leadership Conference or the liberal Protestant groups when those groups set the pattern for such action.

Whatever reservations they had—and many kept the "above politics" outlook—these religious conservatives in effect said, "Never mind from now on," and plunged efficiently into politics. What inspired their foray? Many resented the swing toward pluralism and secularism signaled when the Supreme Court abolished prayer and Bible reading in public schools. A decade later, *Roe* v. *Wade* allowed for choice about abortion and further catalyzed religious conservatives. Moreover, a sense that the mass media were corrupting their young led evangelicals to unite in support of efforts against the distribution of obscene or pornographic materials. "The family" became a social cause, as rates of divorce grew and there were new stresses on families. Feminism, homosexual rights, "big government," and the like inspired the rise of ever more interest groups. Because these social issues came to the fore coincidentally with the burgeoning of evangelical groups on the national scene, these groups' efforts were often more effective at supporting or working against specific candidates or legislation than those of moderate or liberal groups or the denominations.

Today these special-purpose groups formed by conservatives— evangelicals, fundamentalists, Pentecostals, neoevangelicals— display the most political potential. Some analysts say they are the only serious players: few denominations outside this cluster frighten legislators who oppose them because the denominations cannot deliver the votes. Seldom would a candidate appeal for support of, say, Baha'i adherents or Mennonites on election day. And it is difficult to organize individual congregations for causes beyond the local level, though some conservative groups have been learning to do even this. No, the power resides in voluntary associations inspired by religious motives but not connected with specific denominations or formal ecumenical organizations that can control party machinery, pass some legislation, and help elect some candidates and defeat others.

Although the evangelicals on the right drew most notice, they came from an increasingly diverse evangelical cohort. Many evangelicals insisted that various interest groups did not speak for them or draw them to the voting booths. Others disagreed with much in the agenda of leaders on the right. In fact, an "evangelical left" developed in the form of Evangelicals for Social Action.

Among the theses of this book, this fifth one is strongest and clearest: energies are moving from denominations to voluntary associations of people who send in contributions, lend their name to petitions, and go to public meetings, there to be visible in support of the causes they promote or protect. They demand notice.

The Evolution of Interest Groups
and Similar Associations

In the last third of the twentieth century, these agencies attracted the headlines and cameras as no other religious voices did or could. Influential voluntary agencies of religiously motivated and organized people specialized in single issues. Interest groups united to influence voting patterns, pass legislation, and shape morals.

Although interest groups may be misunderstood as *self*-interest groups, readers should in fairness remember that these associations see themselves as *other*-interest groups as well. That is, they often come with a positive vision of what they can do for the kingdom of God, the moral nation, or the good society, and they work to realize elements of their vision.

These interest groups, like all the other organized forms of religious expression in the political sphere, are dynamic agents in a changing society. Their place, their positions, their tactics, and the regard in which they are held is constantly changing. It would be impossible to come up with a definitive understanding of them, but that does not mean that there are no understandings at all.

The Broadening of Interests and Agenda

A key word that comes up on the subject is *broadening*. The Jewish interest "broadened out" from protecting people in the ghetto or under the shadow of discrimination and sought association with other civil libertarian and liberal political forces. One thing most Jews had in common was a fear that public education and other public fronts would promote rites and understandings favoring various concepts of a Christian America.

One way to act on this fear was to guard the line of separation of church and state. Thus for decades, lawyer Leo Pfeffer no doubt spoke for most Jews when he advocated "strict separation." Whenever a church-state case would reach higher courts, one could count on Pfeffer and the American Jewish Committee to guard the ramparts. The AJC warmly supported the Supreme Court in two decisive cases, *Engel* v. *Vitale* (1962) and *Abington School District* v. *Schempp* (1963), which excluded school prayer and devotional Bible reading from public schools. The conservative Protestants who favored public school prayer counterattacked less through denominations and more through voluntary associations. They followed the advice that the best way to oppose an organization is to counterorganize. (As James Madison wrote in *The Federalist*, essays 10 and 51, counterorganization of sect against sect and interest against interest, not legislation, would protect liberties and provide the best ways for groups to gain their modified goals.)

Numbers of Jews in the 1980s became leaders in the Neoconservative movement, and some henceforth turned a critical eye on radical separationism. They looked congenially or even favorably on what an earlier generation would have perceived as violations of church-state separation. They believed that some of the Court activities worked to silence the voices of faith and, in doing so, to promote and privilege a religion of "secularism." Some Neoconservatives began to make common cause with Protestant evangelicals and Catholics who advocated public funding for private schools. The Jewish Neoconservatives did not speak for most American Jews, but enough of them figured prominently in Republican party and administrative affairs, headed foundations or endowments, or had journalistic outlets to alter the picture of Jewish homogeneity in public life. Their odyssey into pluralism and multivocality was typical of what happened in religious groups of all denominations. Each spawned organizations that represented highly focused interests.

Filling a certain vacuum in public life, Jews and others found new outlets and voices in response to the rise of similar interest groups among evangelicals. These Protestants, who account for about one of every four Americans when lumped together by sociologists and statisticians, include fundamentalists, Pentecostals, members of conservative denominations such as the Southern Baptist Convention and the Lutheran Church–Missouri Synod, and others who are comfortable in the National Association of Evangelicals.

Fundraising may be an instrument that motivates such broadening. Organizations may inspire constituents to support one popular cause and then parlay this support into other less glamorous issues. Interest group counteracts interest group: a feminist organization on the left inspires response from the right, which again helps the group on the left raise funds. Such religious interest groups are as tempted as secular ones to exploit anxieties or to engage in imaginative fundraising schemes. They prosper from adversity: when their cause is embattled, they find it easier to rouse support than when all goes well for their cause.

The Politics of Resentment

Broadening in the evangelical camp has tended to occur during a transition in the minds of activists from what we might call the politics of resentment to the politics of will to power. Once dismissed by political and religious elites as "redneck," "Bible Belter," "hillbilly," "backwoods," "holy roller," "fundy," and the like, evangelicals saw gifted spokespersons arise who could exploit the resentment and empower people by helping them speak up, if only, at first, by sending in donations.

This politics of resentment characteristically soon gives way to the politics of will to power. As they experience even a modicum of success, leaders and constituents alike can begin to acquire a taste for exerting ever more influence. Perhaps, they reason, they might even get to "run the show" and reshape America, or at least gain control of one screen in the multiplex of national life. They join up with other groups that were once inspired by resentment but are now growing more confident in their ability to exert power.

Some analysts, like sociologists Robert Wuthnow and Wade Clark Roof, who observe the rise of the new interest groups, also

note that some of the impulse and rhetoric of such groups is anti-
denominational. The groups are not likely to use their leadership
to antagonize congregations, since most of the groups' members are
likely to be members of congregations as well—and quite at home
with them. But the denomination, more remote from day-to-day
experience, can be portrayed negatively to potential interest group
members. Denominations, groups charge, are not "getting it right,"
or they move too slowly; or they have to muffle their prophetic
voices to gain and hold support. They equivocate; they are too moderate; they are inhibited by the internal politics of denominations;
they are afraid to speak out boldly. They have lost their credibility.
But "we," the interest groups, are responsive to and expressive of
our people. "We" can mobilize votes and thus influence the political
process. "We" can produce people who will work patiently with
precinct caucuses, will call on legislators, will work against the can-
didacy of some—as denominations will not or, given tax laws governing nonprofit organizations, cannot.

The most credible answer here, as in the case of individuals,
congregations, and to a lesser extent denominations, is that these
groups have a moral vision, born of their attachment to scriptural
revelation, religious philosophies, tradition, doctrinal statement, or
habit. Because they acquire that vision in subcommunities, they
cannot easily understand or agree with the vision of other groups,
even within the denominations of their members and others with
whom they form coalitions. This approach and understanding
causes interest groups to introduce a feature that is less visible when
individuals or denominations speak up: they cannot negotiate, since
negotiation implies a need to compromise, and compromising is precisely the thing they cannot do. If politics implies a give-and-take,
interest groups cannot participate; they can only step back or find
other ways to recharter society.

Moral vision gives them strength. Even their enemies know they
have to reckon with it. But it also weakens these groups, because
if they cannot compromise with others, they also cannot tolerate

"impurity" within the camp. So there are often doctrinal disputes, ideological tensions, personality clashes, and schisms. They intend to narrow what had been broadened too much. They now must begin again the process of developing, growing, finding coalitions, and broadening.

Strengths of Interest Groups and Voluntary Associations

Characteristically, these groups then issue calls for renewal that would work toward complete reform. They know that (1) there are energies in the public that denominational and ecumenical agencies cannot summon; (2) the interest groups can move more rapidly than denominations can; (3) if they are successful at fundraising and gathering political constituencies, they have to be reckoned with; (4) they will draw media attention while more staid and laid-back religious organizations cannot; and (5) they can promote causes that further polarize society. Whereas churches are burdened down with agendas on causes other than the political, the interest groups, while trading on religious impulses formed for other than political reasons, can focus on issues at hand.

Interest groups are drawn together by people who set examples, take risks, are rhetorically skilled, and can evoke loyalties even as they can describe enemies of their vision in very negative ways. They do not have to worry about "the other half of the congregation" or denomination; their congregation or denomination is ad hoc, made up of the like-minded. And they have another advantage over congregations, denominations, and ecumenical agencies: whereas the traditional institutions must address so much of life, including worship, education, works of mercy, and political engagement, the voluntary associations can be adaptive, brisk, and alert to special signals of public interest or expressions of need. They also, therefore, have more accurate and alert sensors with which to measure social discontents and aspirations. In a sense, it is easier for them to clear their minds and their desks to engage in the cultural conflict immediately before them.

Their dialogues between leaders and respondents and then between those two together and the larger society are part of their strength. Ordinarily, a pastor is chosen for pastoral, not prophetic, skills. A denominational executive is chosen for administrative, not charismatic, characteristics. An ecumenical agent must please many constituencies, not articulate the passions and convictions of one.

Observers note that interest-group leaders represent populist impulses yet often get charged with elitism. They defend themselves by saying that they have much at risk, that they genuinely represent ordinary people—look at the results of the fundraising and mobilizations—and that thus they win credentials even if no one elected them to leadership.

Almost all representatives of interest groups speak of their efficiency and their ability to speak out early, clearly, and without ambiguity on moral and religious themes. When the Gulf War loomed in early 1991, Catholic bishops and other denominations' leaders quietly voiced opposition. Most favored continued negotiation rather than the bombing of civilians and the loss of children's lives. Yet most of these leaders were cautious. They knew that their church membership was of more minds than one, and many of these members did find reason to take military action against Iraq. When the bombing started, the media presented the case in such a way that the population, naturally inclined to back the nation whenever it commits its military forces, found new reasons to close ranks, and the polls showed massive public support for military action. The church leadership was virtually silenced. But the antiwar interest groups were not. They criticized the military, national policy, and media manipulation with no threat of the loss of their constituency, which had gathered specifically to espouse the viewpoints being expressed.

Narrow Issues but a Broad Constituency

Some groups are harder to characterize ideologically. The agency
Bread for the World began with interest in feeding the hungry,
something that Christians, Jews, Muslims, and others unite in supporting. Such things as almsgiving, feeding the poor, and showing
acts of mercy tend to be uncontroversial. But the Bread for the
World leadership soon found that merely sending food did not resolve the situation; it was only a short-term solution. So the group
began to promote related causes, such as development and education. Later it found that some problems it was encountering resulted
from what it regarded as shortcomings in U.S. laws. So group members had to begin lobbying. They turned to individuals and congregations to find advocates who would inundate Congress with letters
promoting changes in policy. This particular organization, like some
others, ultimately divided itself into a tax-exempt educational
agency and a taxed and monitored lobbying group.

The evolution of Bread for the World exemplifies the power and
limitations of interest groups. Whereas antiabortion groups, for example, found it easy to focus on a highly concentrated single issue,
the Bread for the World types had to deal with diffuse issues, disguised enemies, and harder-to-define causes. Yet on the voluntary
organization scene, it, too, thrived.

A Broad but Nonpolarizing Effort

Groups like Bread for the World tend to be far less critical of denominations than the more polarized and polarizing groups tend to
be. Those less critical of denominations in effect urge the congregations to acquire a full agenda, a larger scope, and greater competence at ministering to the care of souls. When such congregations
are healthy, they will produce groups of people who will step beyond
the local instruments and find or be found by interest groups, which
will serve to instruct them on issues that might not otherwise have

mattered to them but turn out to be congruent with their religious message and beliefs.

Whereas the more extreme groups might antagonize traditional religious organizations, those that are less polarizing are usually perceived (and position themselves) as instruments that can supplement congregational life. Their leaders often explicitly ask, "What can we do that congregations and denominations cannot?" and then focus on supplying answers. They also may spare leaders of denominations some agony, because when there is controversy, it will be the outside organization that takes the heat, not denominational ministers or executives.

As these examples make clear, religious voluntary associations are theologically varied, specialized in their approaches, and restless with denominational leadership, but they are prepared to go into action only when they are certain of unambivalent support.

From Self-Interest to Interest

Interest groups or voluntary organizations form on the political front at different stages in the life of religious groups. In the earliest stages after immigration or formation, most members have to work out of self-interest, protecting their group and those in it. This would today be characteristic of many American Muslim organizations. They are finding that as their membership grows, they have to hear and present many voices. Thus Islamic feminists begin to speak and to find support in interest groups. It is likely that the Muslim antidefamation leagues and their kin will soon replicate what Jewish and Christian groups had earlier produced, for it is difficult to influence political life without such agencies.

Voluntary associations cannot permanently avoid all the problems that beset denominational and ecumenical life. In a political society, it is hard to set forth a vision of the kingdom of God or of a productive society without finding that almost all issues and approaches have been thought of in the secular and usually more pluralistic political parties. Speak for this Bread for the World policy or that one of the Christian Coalition, and you find that you are immediately typed as "Democratic" or "Republican." But on the voluntary association front, unlike the denominational one, such partisan identification involves somewhat less risk. The interest groups may help create tension in parties and divide their factions and leadership, but they are unlikely to divide themselves. A religious homosexual rights organization will link with the political party that is most likely to act on the group's vision, and doing so will not cost the group a single member. A denomination that does the same greatly risks losing adherents. In a partisan society, then, interest groups have the advantage of being more efficient and representative than inherited institutions.

These interest groups do not always specialize and compete with denominations or with each other. Their leadership can often help define public issues in new ways and motivate their followers without distancing themselves from others. Thus they contribute to society's pool of moral energy even if they do not agree among themselves.

Some observers point out that voluntary associations often do break ranks but then make precedents for denominations that would follow them. Thus antiabortion forces chided many denominations that had insisted that they never took political stands. Members and leaders in such church bodies became convinced that by their silence they were contributing to murderous national policies. They began to speak out on this issue. If they garnered massive support on one such cause, they might move into other areas. Thus in the 1980s and 1990s, the Christian Life Commission of the Southern Baptist Convention, alerted by independent interest groups, grew bolder in its venture into politics. It is doubtful that new commission leadership would have done so had it not been convinced that most members of the convention already agreed with various stands, which matched those of more freewheeling voluntary interest groups who had been there first.

We have already illustrated this by reference to family issues, but the theme bears elaboration. After the middle of the twentieth century, many challenges rose to the family, however defined. The birth control pill made it possible for more women to restrict their childbearing and to work outside the home. But whether women found fulfillment on the job, felt it necessary to earn money to supplement family income, or found themselves raising children on their own, they experienced strain in married and family life. Popular culture advocated lifestyles that drew young people and married couples into sexual experimentation. Divorce rates grew. Many young people in rebellion repudiated traditional family ways.

Liberals grieved as much as anyone else when their young became alienated. They suffered as much when unwanted divorce occurred. They had to adapt to drastic changes in the sexual ethos. But they did not have instrumentalities to organize them and their thinking. Meanwhile, as evangelicals and other conservatives faced all the same cultural threats and possibilities, they did decide to resist or adapt more creatively than mainstream secular, Catholic, Jewish, and other Protestant groups did. They invented pro-family groups. As moderates and liberals witnessed these successes, they formed groups that interacted with evangelicals and conservative Catholics. One might cite the Institute for American Values, which produced initiatives that drew scholarly attention to fatherhood and convoked the Council on the Family. Out of such efforts came more sentiment for doing something about family disintegration— perhaps more clarified because conservatives had been there first.

Society's Perception of Voluntary Agencies

How does society perceive voluntary agencies? Here one must draw a line between agencies of justice, all of which have immediate political consequences, and agencies of mercy, which thrive on more indirect relations to partisan causes. Thus antiwar activities, however motivated they were and are by specific faith-based impulses,

immediately drew the voluntary groups into political confronta-
tions. Similarly, antiabortion fronts prosper only to the degree that
they can form partisan political alliances. Causes such as refugee resettlement may be born of mercy, but given voter differences over
immigration issues, they are soon involved in political situations.
Even the mildest form of charitable activity tends to involve the religious in politics, especially given that they are often stewards of
tax funds. The Salvation Army, immigration resettlement agencies,
and world relief organizations all tend to raise their own funds even
as they administer programs related to revenue bases.

In a political society, it is hard to effect any kind of change without coming up against political forces. What many sensitive as well
as aggressive religious leaders forget is that when they enter the political arena, no one will show them respect simply because they are
religious. They are instead perceived as political players among the
other political players. Sometimes they may even evoke a special
measure of opposition from those who resent the claim that God is
on one side or another. Religion that "goes public" in the political
order both earns and risks religious capital.

Anomalies abound on this front. In many Iowa communities,
for instance, mainstream Protestant churches put considerable energy into ineffective efforts to forbid casino gambling. People in
their communities who would profit from employment or management of gambling places had to fight these religious groups in legislatures. Their religious opponents acted out of tax-free charitable
institutions, a point never lost on their antagonists. Tax-free church
bodies that avoided investment participation in companies that did
business in South Africa during apartheid temporarily harmed the
interests of American corporations—and did so from tax-free bases,
even if their actions cost nonbelievers or others who had different
views of the effectiveness of economic boycotts.

In a money economy, the interest groups have to raise funds to
support political activities. The congregations and denominations
do their fundraising in ways that diffuse political effects. People give
for the whole cause, part of which they budget for political con-

cerns. This fact leads many to be cautious and leads others into great internal controversy.

The interest groups do not have that problem. They wield power while flaunting the fact that donations to their cause are in effect votes of confidence. Congress and other political actors can gauge the potential effects of an agency's power by the size of its budget and the amount and sources of donated funds. The groups encourage the impression that their funding increases their political clout—and not necessarily just to impress the politicians. The intent is also to attract supportive constituencies that will then wield power on many levels.

Precisely what the resources are and how they are used in the interest groups can reveal the kind of power they will have. Are the politically minded actors perceived to be acting on the basis of profound, durable scriptures, traditions, communities, and expressions? Or are they "making it up as they go along," suddenly adapting scriptures to the political moment? In the 1960s, certain ecumenical and denominational agencies and leaders lost credibility when members seemed to be acting reflexively, more out of obeisance to some outdated religious model than out of a deep personal commitment. They were dismissed as "Sunday soldiers," people without staying power. The harsh judgments may not have been fair, but a great many of them did indeed disappear after their moment in the sun.

Decades later, it is becoming clear that on the left and the right alike, the quest for power and the necessity of coalition can lead to a displacement of specifically religious conviction or explicitness. The specifically religious agenda gets obscured and the faith-based voice often becomes muted so as not to alienate allies of other faiths who share the cause but not the theological conviction. The mainstream churches experienced this diffusing and refocusing some time ago. Now evangelical movements such as the Christian Coalition draw suspicion in the eyes of those who see them as "mere" political actors who leave their religious commitments behind or distort them for tactical purposes.

The larger citizenry evidently both wants the religious groups to be explicitly religious—as the public defines religiousness—and has trouble identifying with those that invoke the scriptures and texts of faiths other than their own and then try to impose their readings on people of other religious persuasions.

The Need for Enemies—and Friends

"Mass movements can rise and spread without a belief in a God, but never without belief in a devil," wrote longshoreman-philosopher Eric Hoffer.[1] Interest groups also prosper when they have clearly defined enemies.

Often a Manichaean instinct motivates those who would mobilize others for the cause: this one, they contend, is simply a situation of "us" versus "them," God versus Satan, or Christ versus Antichrist. In the minds of such mobilizers, there is little room for ambiguity, reserve, complexity, or internal contradiction. When such groups win too much power and get too involved with the society, they also find it harder to hold themselves together.

Some sociologists have listened to mainstream Protestants moan about decline and answer, in effect, "What are you complaining about? You won!" Enough of their program got implemented, at least since the beginning of the New Deal, to sap energies that would have gone into their becoming or remaining oppositional against all cultural signs and stances. They also ran out of foes. The ecumenical movement deprived them of Roman Catholicism as the enemy against which they could mobilize. The more effective voluntary agencies energetically portray their enemies in the grossest terms possible: the secular humanist, the liberal, the relativist, the compromiser, the moderate, the fundamentalist.

Mention of the waxing and waning of power, as in the case of mainstream causes over conservative Catholic, Neoconservative Jewish, and evangelical Protestant forces, occasions questions about the cultural contexts of such movements. How influenced are each of them by causes that originate outside themselves and then become fashionable, winnable, or easily addressed? Many churches opposed the legalization of gambling. As legal gambling started to make its way through state lotteries and revenue- and job-producing casinos in otherwise depressed areas, the public, including the religious public, generally came to support the legalization of gambling and even governmental support of it. But by and large, neither the organized denominations nor the interest groups presented much of a front against the legitimation and legalization of such. So the question arises, Has religion lost its shaping power, when even special-purpose groups in its name begin to fade away?

Another version of the question goes as follows: the prosperity of public religion and of religious groups acting in public coincides with what many claim is a revival of religion. It may be hard to think of a time in the last half century when someone somewhere did not make credible claims that there was a religious revival going on. But the revivals have taken numerous forms through those decades. Today the religious revival is most evident in the sphere of unanchored, noncommunal, often anti–organized religion probes among "spirituality minded" people who cannot be called on to support causes. But observers match these impulses with some communal impulses among those who would effect change.

The Future of Special-Purpose Groups

Did the purported revival make the groups possible, or did the groups help stimulate the revival? Such questions get asked as politicians and governmental leaders assess how much hearing they should give to the articulate voices and organized groups. Will they adapt for them now, only to be left behind tomorrow?

The various generations alive today display a variety of attitudes on this front. The younger generations, which place a higher value on personal experience than on organizational affiliation, will more likely respond to immediate ad hoc appeals. There are whole

congregations based on market research that will reach the individuals who "pick and choose" churches and prefer "religion à la
carte." Will the recruits stay around and remain loyal through the
next generation or two or three? The older interest groups are especially busy learning how to adapt to an environment in which
loyalties are shallow and short-lived.

Some observers contend that whereas the older generations
bring more vestiges of the ideology of left and right to causes, the
younger ones will do little doctrinal probing or fighting. They may
engage in immediate activity for a cause that involves them with
the political scene. But they may not reason out how to change the
political order. Instead they might give to or work at a food bank
without always realizing how food banks connect to the larger world
of politics. So interest groups progressively come to involve themselves in educational and community-building work.

One by-product of this educational work has an antennalike
character. The highly mobile, market-driven, sensitive, and immediately responsive interest groups often catch disturbing signals or
opportunities early and react early. In the course of time, more moderate ones do the same. Such a dynamic is evident in the way pro-
family groups alerted the larger culture to address issues relating to
fatherhood, teenage pregnancy, and the like. Some pro-environment
groups began to use religious resources to take on ecological concerns and were first dismissed as extremists. Inevitably, they were
drawn into international, domestic, and local politics, since environmental concerns eventually demand budgets, rearrangement of
priorities, and political negotiation. But even if they did not pull
the larger religious constituency into agreement, they did force more
people to find ways to address the issue.

A More Accurate Picture of Secular America

The more that representatives and observers of the interest groups
speak up and appraise the situation, the more one can see the need
to revise the claims that the public square is devoid of religious sym-

bols and signals and the political order has trivialized religion in a culture of disbelief. Many a legislator will say that the public forum is instead festooned with religious banners and displays them as the various cause supporters march to the doors of legislators or try to influence voting. Many who may once have trivialized religion now know they have to keep their guard up, since religious interest groups can "do them in" if they are not careful. Others drop their guard and run up to the religious groups for the sake of the power they represent. There is no claim here that "secular society" or religiously neutral political and governmental orders are on the point of disappearing. The claim is simply that America is a religiosecular society, a place where lines between church and state are increasingly blurred thanks to such interest groups. The boundaries of the zones marked sacred and profane are not so easily discernible as they once were.

Evidently, religious groups are struggling to find new ways in a pluralistic society to act on convictions and build in politics while not bartering away the assets that have animated them to date. They do this in a variety of ways. Thus the African American churches, long unobserved by the rest of American religious groups, continue to pursue what have come to be called "faith-based" ventures. These involve some usually carefully circumscribed alliances with metropolitan governments. They may deal with sectors of the city that everyone else, public and private, religious and secular, official and voluntary, has abandoned. For example, they get governmental authorities to invest in apartment buildings that they will maintain and where they will teach the homeless how to be "homed." They could not do this without the help of taxing bodies, in actions that will look like transgressions of the boundaries of church and state, yet the ethically sensitive among them take care to do no explicit evangelizing or proclaiming among the people they serve.

In the course of time, nonblack religious groups learn from this and begin to take more favorable views of the "faith-based"—to the point that by 1999, political candidates in both parties were allying with such organizations and moves.

Such groups have become, along the way, part of the leadership of voluntary associational life. More than half of adult Americans volunteer time and energies for a cause. More than half of them do their volunteering through religious organizations or on religious impulses. They are showing that the government is not the only forum where profound issues can be addressed and fought over. But leaders of volunteer groups also are learning that most of them are not likely to be able to advance their agenda without finding ways to work with other religious groups and, selectively, with government and politicians to help them start the conversation or effect a desirable end.

Because mainstream Protestantism, organized Catholicism, and Reform and Conservative Judaism during the second half of the twentieth century were finding ways to work together and to address the common good, a weakening of their voice and a further weakening of their base could become problematic for them. Many of the interest groups of the religiously fervent—Orthodox Judaism, Islam, conservative Catholicism, and the evangelical-Pentecostal-fundamentalist cohort—have moved to the front in efforts to effect change in society. As they build coalitions and enjoy some success, it seems appropriate to ask, Are they now also on the way to "mainline" status, with all the assets and liabilities that that implies? Will they invent new ways to relate to the political order, or will they be dismissed, as some of them are now being dismissed, as mere political manipulators who use religion in pursuit of power? Can one form a republic among intense religious groups without some politically minded negotiators, compromisers, and "live and let live" types among them? There are some signs, from evangelical-Jewish and Catholic-evangelical circles, that old ignorances and animosities decline as some coalition builders from each side engage in probes of the other and in common action with them.

The Future: Good Things

At the same time, most interest groups will in the end draw on the energies of particular traditions. Many Catholics moved from the starting point, advocacy of better ways for immigrants, through cautious acceptance in the mainstream to the point where today Catholics, on the left and the right alike, can draw on papal social documents of the past century and try to bring them to bear on the body politic. African American churches will continue to remain powers on the congregational level, even as they learn the need for more interest groups to represent their cause and the cause of justice. Evangelicals and Mormons are trying to mine their scriptures and traditions for accents that will stay with them through contradictory social changes.

Some chroniclers suggest that even if formal systematic theological enterprises do not draw large constituencies today, on the ethical front there is much vitality. One thinks of the contributions to medical care and ethics by people who try to discern religious meanings in care and cure. These come from people who draw on sacred traditions—and then, to effect change, from people who must work within the political order, where they are likely to awaken opposition. They are forced to think about their deepest commitments, and they often get a chance to describe these to the larger community. So the main accents of interest groups can quite naturally indicate what kinds of religious renewal are going on in various times.

We are beginning to see the development of this kind of renewal on a long-neglected front. At the century's end, after the free market had "won out" over the collectivist and aggressive welfare societies, it began occurring to many observers that the market exacts a price for its successful functioning. The gap between rich nations and poor, rich people and poor, grows drastically, to the point that it impels a search for fresh perspectives. The amassing of huge fortunes by the ungenerous has led to questioning by people who worry about those left behind by welfare reform and those who need programs and subsidies. Much criticism of these comes from religious sources. The cost to the human spirit of lives reduced to competition and consumerism worries religious leaders, from the pope to the local pastor who counsels individuals and families torn apart by the developments. As awareness of all this grows, religious groups do more to provide counsel, retreats, alternatives, empathy, and programs as one small step in writing scenarios for ways to make the market order more humane. As they do so, they draw on profound religious resources and thus demonstrate another dimension of religious renewal.

What Special-Purpose Groups Bring to the Public Forum

Some religious groups have benefited from once-feared pluralistic encounters in the world of volunteerism. Protestant conservatives used to insist that their only business was to save souls and prepare them for heaven and shunned controversial religious addresses to people's physical needs. Today it seems unnecessary to fight such battles. Almost all who are in religious groups agree that people who act on the basis of faith-based impulses must feed the poor. The question of how best to do this plunges them back into politics. If old fundamentalist-modernist conflicts from the 1920s to the 1970s drove away many wary and exhausted partisans, many are getting over this. They are refocusing not on their churchly enemies but on human need that is apparent to all sides, though they may address it in different ways. In the process, they look at long-neglected sources in their own traditions and borrow from others.

Some will be led to movements on the political and economic left, and some will join movements to the right. To some observers, this duality speaks to the weakness of religion: Why not have leaders get their act together before they appeal to others? To others, the result adds to futility: two sets of Baptists, both in the name of God, claim to have a vision and directions for where to go. Won't they cancel each other out? The purely pragmatic politician might think so. But people who are concerned about moral, theological, intellectual, and spiritual depth are more likely to welcome contentiousness and conversations that draw on resources of which society would otherwise be ignorant or deprived.

It may be that the prosperity of interest groups may lead to ever more public suspicion, weariness, and wariness as they fight among themselves. It may also happen that new coalitions will constantly form in a self-reforming process. What is certain is that they will meet criticism from others, criticism of the sort that James Madison thought would enliven the body politic. They will at the very least have enlarged their repertoire of options for dealing with problems.

In any case, the surprising realignments that have occurred since the 1970s suggest that the new century will be dynamic and full of change in this anything but merely secular republic.

Types of Power

It is clear by now that no single religious approach or voice holds sway in politics or government. Religions long on the scene—Protestants of the mainstream, for example, or groups that bring internationally based resolutions, such as Catholics moved by papal documents—all employ similar approaches. The smaller movements, once called sectarian, such as the peace churches—Mennonites and Church of the Brethren, among others—have their own distinctive approaches. They may be able to be more radical, more focused, more homogeneous: one joins such a group precisely because of its tight focus. The very multivocality of denominations and religious movements in America furthers the formation of interest groups within and around them. The groups do not have to keep a whole traditional agenda and range of concerns in mind; they can focus on one front at a time. Whichever approach they take, these special-interest groups remain today the conduits through which most religious people funnel their political energies.

6

An Invitation to All Religious People
Join the Political Conversation

Thesis: It is important for the common good for religious people to join the political conversation—and get involved.

Throughout this book, I have used *we* so as to include not only the editorial and research team that helped put this manuscript together but also the Public Religion Project, which I directed and which hosted a series of conversations about politics and religion—conversations out of which this book grew. But in this chapter, I am going to speak only for myself. I do not want to be inhibited by concern that my argument here has the endorsement of the Project staff, its advisory board, the Pew Charitable Trusts (which funded the Public Religion Project and its endeavors), the University of Chicago (which hosted the Project), or the participants in the conversations we sponsored.

In other words, I am going to "take the gloves off" and push for conclusions, action, and new directions.

I hope that while reading this book, you've felt as if at a party of people who share a common interest, all caught up in animated conversation. We will not finish the conversation in this chapter, for conversation is always open-ended, and religion and politics are always dynamic and changing. I will instead turn it over to you and the others.

The Internal Conversation and Conflict

The course of your conversation is unpredictable. It may involve working ideas out with others, or it may be entirely internal, simply turning things over in your mind. And it will be never-ending: so many issues about politics and religion are so complex and have so many sides that they seldom get resolved. Only a pure ideologue has an answer for everything. Only someone without a sense of history can stay stuck with a political creed no matter what the circumstances.

Let me illustrate. Sometimes when the courts act, I am thankful that I do not have to make the decision, as in the following case. The plight of the daughter of a Christian Scientist couple is brought to the court's attention. According to all medical counsel, the child will die if not given a specific medical treatment. But the girl's loving, pious, caring, conscientious parents refuse, on the grounds that the medical procedure will violate their deep religious faith and commitments. The spiritual side of my brain says, "Nothing is more important than the free exercise of religion. Give the government even the slightest opening to declare what is legitimate in religion, and you have lost your most cherished freedom." The parental side of my brain says, "Nothing is more important than saving the life of a child, especially one who has no say in a decision that can end her life or give her a future." The members of the court may be enduring the same mental conversing, arguing, warring, and questioning, but they must act. And they must act fast. They do not have the luxury of citizens like us, conversing with ourselves in an unending internal dialogue.

Here is another illustration. A fundamentalist university is threatened with the loss of all federal aid to students and programs if it does not follow all federal guidelines regarding the interaction of people of different races. This school teaches, incredibly to me, that the Bible that it must follow teaches segregation and "separate development" of races. The case comes to the courts. One set of voices in this internal conversation speaks up for the intent of the federal program and finds the belief of the university's sponsoring group reprehensible. The other set of voices in my head speaks up for the freedom of the religious group to do its own biblical interpretation. It is not threatening the foundation of the republic, leading a revolution, bearing arms, or turning anarchist. The group is patriotic and law-abiding in other areas. How should one rule on this? Let the conversation go on; there will be analogous cases in the future.

A third illustration comes from the realm of social policy. When I was a boy in the Depression era, the rights of labor were only beginning to be assured. The New Deal advanced them, and from the 1930s through the 1950s, there were intense and plausible arguments that had to do with the rights of labor to organize and to strike. There were legislative battles over the "closed shop" just as today there are battles about the use of union funds to represent the unions in legislative lobbying and in attracting voters to support specific pro-labor candidates. In those days, labor as an organized movement was on the defensive, often small and weak and unprotected. So one of the voices within me seconded the call of the heart to support laborers and labor, people I knew and I knew to be on the short end of the stick in labor-management interactions. And there were plenty of religious warrants for such support of the relatively powerless and the obviously put-upon.

Times changed, and three decades later it was obvious that labor had become Big Labor, often to match in power, self-centeredness, and sometimes in corruption the Big Management it had been opposing. It was not time to jump off the labor wagon; too many rights were at stake, too many jobs and valid practices. But now another voice within me says, "Be careful. Take a second look. Notice all sides. See how labor has turned in on itself, often unmindful of the needs of others and working to preserve the power of its leadership at the expense of inconvenienced citizens." Henceforth I have to keep the prophets in mind, eyes wide open, and a sense of balance as religion and politics meet on this issue.

Another illustration could be welfare and welfare reform. Beginning with Roosevelt's New Deal and then following through Kennedy's New Frontier and Johnson's Great Society, it became clear that Americans had to think through the questions having to do with the welfare of all citizens. An affluent society was overlooking and adding to the problems of "the other America." There were plenty of warrants in the biblical tradition and the version of it that comes through my religious tradition for mobilization against poverty, oppression, and neglect. That meant, in an age when no other agency was poised to tackle the issue, that government had to be involved somehow. The result: a moderate welfare society. "Hooray!" is the reaction from the endorsing side of mind and mouth.

Then, as decades pass, we find that the welfare system has itself become inequitable, often unmonitored, sometimes corrupt. For many people, it has become a way of life, an instrument that promotes dependence and destroys initiative. Using the same sacred books as before, I found it important to revisit the scene and support some measure of welfare reform, imperfect as that measure may be. Yet the pro-reform voices are not final or fully convincing. Many other kinds of reform are still needed.

Have I changed convictions in the case of the religious parents and their freedom, the segregationist academy, the rights of labor, or the need for welfare? No, though I am ready to be convinced of the need for change and ready to be moved toward that change as the result of conversation and argument. Instead, having heard the testimony of others and having been challenged by them, I take new evidence into consideration and act on the basis of it.

In the end, my representatives in federal and state government have to vote yes or no on legislation. That means that the various sides of the brain must turn to the matter of public policy, and the voices within have to yield to one voice, that of the person who must act. Were I a juror on a controverted case, I could not say "Half guilty" or "Between innocence and guilt" or "There's much to say on all sides." I'd have to vote "Guilty" or "Not guilty" and let the jury conversation end.

Conversation in the Community

The foregoing consideration of the personal perspective is a way of saying that conversation always begins in the mind and heart and soul of the citizen-believer. But the larger conversation is not limited to this argument with the self. We have pictured it going on in various small and large circles. It belongs in a gathering of people in adult classes or meetings in a congregation. It belongs in a community whose school board will face difficult decisions. Let library board members take it up. Perhaps a college classroom is the locale, or a Parent-Teacher Association or a voluntary group.

Religious Groups' Engagement with Politics and Government

This book, in laying the framework for such conversations, has highlighted the concerns some people rightfully have about religion's place in the political sphere. Yet I reiterate here that although religion is in some dimensions a private affair, it also belongs in public affairs. Religion is a part of ordinary life: the workplace, the worlds of friendly interaction, the mall, the academy, the media, the gallery. But it takes on special importance in the political realm.

That is why the voices of religion should be in the public forum and at the political table, for reasons like the following, some of which will by now be familiar.

Religion Will Not Go Away

The call to get rid of religion will be ineffectual, pointless, and distracting from other calls and questions that have some chance of being effective, to the point, and focused. Despite three modern centuries of "enlightenment," skepticism, questioning, challenge, and the offering of nonreligious competition, religion around the world is prospering and its forces are expanding. In Europe not much is happening, but Africa, Asia, Latin America, and most of North America are hearing more of religion than before. The search for meaning, the passions of the heart, the demands of soul are too strong to let the human race stop asking religious questions. And so long as billions do, it is important to ask not "How do we get rid of it?" but "What do we do with what is here?"

Consider the Alternatives

In the Enlightenment, new horrors replaced those of corrupt and unthinking priestcraft. New nationalisms came to produce something that looked like creeds. And they came with weaponry and the impulse to war to support their claims. The isms of the twentieth century—fascism, Nazism, communism, Maoism, and others—set out to stamp out religion and come up with new ideologies that looked like religions. Every dictator had the same instinct: kill the priests, put barbed wire around religious dissenters. The religious call on God and are comforted in distress by God, the dictators reasoned, and so the more you set out to replace their religion, the more their faith rides them through; they must be kept away from the rest of the population.

A Republic Prospers When Many Voices Speak

James Madison, in *The Federalist*, believed this. He worried most, as some of us do today, that one kind of religious voice—that of the left in the 1960s, of the right in the 1990s—would be most highly motivated, effective, and successful. Could one of these forces come to predominance and work toward the end of the republican venture we have known? The best way to ward that off, says Madison, is to count on opposing religious voices to be "jealous" for their opinions and consequently to counterorganize. You don't like the Christian Coalition? You counterorganize, just as it got started as a counterorganizing force. You think Jewish lobbies have too much influence on U.S. policy? You organize other voices. The outcome will not be holy war but a reckoning with more viewpoints.

Politics Doesn't Divide Religious Groups; Warfare Does

When religious groups learn the rules of the game of politics, which are themselves messy, they learn that they must make room for conflict but not let it destroy the institution in which it is expressed. When denominations or congregations allow for free and open debate and keep the covenant not to exclude the "other" or the dissenter, they become more vigorous. When a force within them turns warlike and authoritarian and says, in effect, "Shape up or ship out!" politics ends, warfare begins, schism results, and winners take all— or all that is left.

People Should Use the Best Resources Available to Them

For religious people, mobilizing their best resources means reaching into the recesses and treasures of faith, subjecting the passing parade to careful analysis, and seeking perspective, perhaps an old one, perhaps a new one. Religion will not have a monopoly except in the zealot's heart. In everyone else, it will have its place alongside concerns for the economy, one's health, educational institutions, safety from criminals, and devotion to this or that political philosophy. And it can play a positive role in countering other forces: political parties, government as a set of remote bureaucracies, commerce and business, the media and entertainment. All of these can become encompassing expressions of power over mind and heart, soul and body.

Politics Needs Reinvigoration

Elections have become auctions, as donors or investors buy candidates and lobby for policies that serve the minority. Religious groups, many of them African American, have shown that something as simple (but demanding) as registering voters and getting them to go to the polls can change the dynamics. Politics used to have drive and focus, and religion seemed passive. Today politics breeds apathy, but where religion is dynamic—as it often is—it helps rouse people from apathy to see worldly concerns in a new light.

Religious People Can Delimit the Political Order

We often act as if our republics, our parties, and our causes are eternal and can take the place of the Ultimate. The word of faith reminds us that we are temporal and finite and that spiritual concerns transcend the political issues of the day. Awareness of that can liberate politics and let it serve the large and rightful place it holds in the scheme of things.

Civility and Public Religion

I am aware of hazards in setting forth each of those arguments against the antireligious and the religious privatists. If religion ("faith," "spirituality") is to have its place in the public order, including its witness in politics and government, it will need reform. But I think this reform is more likely if a wide range of religious interests are present. They force all to examine themselves, to reexplore their testimony, to ask what compromises are worthwhile to the religious group and valuable in the political order, and to follow the rules of the game for religion in American politics.

The rules of the game that get frequently, even characteristically, broken have to do with what passes under the code word *civility*. The Public Religion Project out of which this book grew was chartered in no small measure to face up to the problem of incivility among religious groups. That charter sought to respond to the observation that publics could proceed rather far in a political debate until the religious factions were heard. Then the debates often turned zealous, fanatical, unthinking, unhearing—at least to outside observers. Religious factions had to learn to be civil for the sake of the integrity of faith, the political process, regard for other people, and the republic.

Even so, never expect political talk, religiously inspired or not, to be simply or serenely civil to the point that it "sinks into decent politeness." Different interests, creeds, and personalities will be involved, and they will bring passion. Rather, the goal of the conversation is to help people envision and practice ways for those of good intentions to be true to themselves, their faiths, their causes—and do little damage to others along the way.

That is a rather limited way to speak of a process that has considerable promise for the republic. At the beginning of the third millennium, citizens as believers and citizens in general need all the help they can get putting to work the various mediating structures of society that do so much to enliven it.

Where to Begin?

No one can be expert in or committed to many causes. Anyone can be spread too thin and become enervated. So where does one begin?

Some people may choose to establish forums that will deal with the cost of the market economy of which we are now a part. These have political dimensions that have to do with foreign aid, trade relations, priorities that affect everyone from Kansas wheat farmers to Wall Street traders.

Others may get engaged in political causes that have to do with the environment. Most religious bodies have agencies that deal with these issues, and congregations can start them. Whether or not we survive will depend in no small part on decisions made during the next generation. Religious groups all have something to say about the natural world and the temporal order. Are their adherents visiting these resources? Is anyone out there who is despoiling the environment being inconvenienced by religious groups?

An aging society poses tremendous political issues, and the various scriptures show great concern for the aged and their needs. No individual or congregation is too small or denomination or ecumenical or interest group too large to escape the burdens of this subject.

Three out of four Americans list education as their first or second issue of concern at the turn of the millennium. Education is an intensely political realm. Did you ever run for the local school board? Religious interests are at stake. Does your school board hear from no religious groups, or has it heard too much from one kind? This is both a close-up issue for small groups in local communities and a matter of national priorities and policies.

Prosperity, health care, and reasonable security are not available for at least one-fifth of Americans. Neither rural nor urban America offers a place to hide from the issue, though the prosperous may have found ways to hide the victims. Again, the existence of such an underclass is a religious issue, to be faced with a variety of strategies and arguments. Is a conversation and plan of action going on in your circles to deal with at least local dimensions of the problem?

Religious voices have much to say on the questions of delivery of health care. These are political issues with religious dimensions.

I could extend this list indefinitely. I begin each morning by reading two newspapers, always with "religion and public life" items in mind, and find five to ten clear instances per day. I do not pretend that the world would be better off if 260 million citizens suddenly "religiosify" every issue and bring spiritual passion to every cause. I certainly do not think that religion prospers when people are merely busy, running around and speaking out on all fronts. I do think that religion can sometimes do more harm than good in politics and government and I often cringe at some of the political sermonizing I hear blaring from the lips of religious leaders.

I do believe, however, that the way to sort out the trivial from the urgent and the appropriate from the irrelevant is getting a variety of people together and starting a conversation. That's a technique suggested by a civil rights leader in Chicago more than three decades ago: "We just get a roomful of people," he explained, "and tell them not to come out until they have a solution." "To what problem?" "You'll find out quickly enough if you only start talking."

So start talking.

Notes

Introduction

1. Sebastian de Grazia, "Under God?" *Times Literary Supplement*, June 4, 1999, pp. 13–14.

2. All quotations from Eugene E. Brussell (ed.), *Dictionary of Quotable Definitions* (Upper Saddle River, N.J.: Prentice Hall, 1970), pp. 447–448.

3. Bernard Crick, *In Defence of Politics* (Chicago: University of Chicago Press, 1962), pp. 140–141.

4. Peter Berger, *The Sacred Canopy* (New York: Doubleday, 1967).

5. Brussell, pp. 485–490.

6. Paul Tillich, *Systematic Theology*, Vol. 1 (Chicago: University of Chicago Press, 1951), pp. 11–12, 14.

7. Benjamin Franklin, "Proposals Relating to the Education of Youth in Philadelphia." In Chester E. Jorgenson and Frank Luther Mott (eds.), *Benjamin Franklin: Selections* (New York: Hill & Wang, 1962), p. 203.

8. Thomas Gilbey, quoted in John Courtney Murray, *We Hold These Truths: Catholic Reflections on the American Proposition* (New York: Sheed & Ward, 1960), p. 6.

9. Murray, *We Hold These Truths*, p. 9

10. Murray, *We Hold These Truths*, p. 9.

11. Murray, *We Hold These Truths*, p. 9.

12. David Tracy, *Plurality and Ambiguity: Hermeneutics, Religion, Hope* (San Francisco: HarperSanFrancisco, 1987), p. 18.

13. Tracy, *Plurality and Ambiguity*, p. 18.

14. Tracy, *Plurality and Ambiguity*, p. 19.

Chapter One

1. John Winthrop, *The Winthrop Papers*, 5 vols., ed. A. B. Forbes (Boston: 1964–67), 2:293.

2. T. B. Maston, *Isaac Backus: Pioneer of Religious Liberty* (Rochester, N.Y.: American Baptist Historical Society, 1962), pp. 78–79.

3. Alan Wolfe, *One National After All: What Middle-Class Americans Really Think About God, Country, Family, Racism, Welfare, Immigration, Homosexuality, Work, the Right, the Left, and Each Other* (New York: Viking, 1998), p. 72.

4. Brian K. Smith, "Monotheism and Its Discontents: Religious Violence and the Bible," *Journal of the American Academy of Religion* 66, (1998): 403–411.

5. Regina M. Schwarz, *The Curse of Cain: The Violent Legacy of Monotheism* (Chicago: University of Chicago Press, 1997), p. 5.

6. Deborah Manley (ed.), *The Guinness Book of Records, 1492: The World Five Hundred Years Ago* (New York: Facts on File, 1992), p. 166.

7. Peter Berkowitz, "Thou Shalt Not Kill," *New Republic*, June 23, 1997, p. 42.

8. Gabriel A. Almond, Emmanuel Sivan, and R. Scott Appleby, "Explaining Fundamentalism." In Martin E. Marty and R. Scott Appleby (eds.), *Fundamentalism Comprehended* (Chicago: University of Chicago Press, 1995), p. 429.

9. Almond, Sivan, and Appleby, "Explaining Fundamentalism," p. 402.

10. John Leland, *Rights of Conscience and Therefore Religious Opinions Not Cognizable by Law* (1791).

Chapter Two

1. Hans Kuitert, *Everything Is Politics, but Politics Is Not Everything: A Theological Perspective on Faith and Politics* (Grand Rapids, Mich.: Eerdmans, 1986).

2. Glenn Tinder, *The Political Meaning of Christianity* (San Francisco: HarperSanFrancisco, 1991), ch. 1.

Chapter Three

1. Robert Frost, "Build Soil: A Political Pastoral." In Edward Lathem (ed.), *The Poetry of Robert Frost: The Collected Poems, Complete and Unabridged* (New York: Henry Holt, 1979), p. 324.

2. Richard Nixon, quoted in Charles P. Henderson Jr., *The Nixon Theology* (New York: HarperCollins, 1972), p. 135.

3. Jimmy Carter, *Living Faith* (New York: Times Books, 1996), p. 125.

4. See Richard P. McBrien, *Caesar's Coin: Religion and Politics in America* (Old Tappan, N.J.: Macmillan, 1987), pp. 34–35, 151–155.

Chapter Four

1. Stephen Toulmin, *Cosmopolis: The Hidden Agenda of Modernity* (New York: Free Press, 1990).

2. For instance, in the United Methodist Church, 81.2 cents go to local needs; 14.2 cents go to district, region, and multistate jurisdictions; and 4.5 cents go to national and international ministries; Thomas S. McAnally, "'Apportionments' Represent Ministries Around the World," *United Methodist News Service,* Apr. 2, 1998.

3. Paul Ramsey, *Who Speaks for the Churches?* (Nashville, Tenn.: Abingdon Press, 1967).

4. Mark A. Chaves, "Secularization in the Twentieth-Century United States." Ph.D. thesis, Harvard University.

5. A. James Reichley, *Religion in American Public Life* (Washington, D.C.: The Brookings Institution, 1985), p. 251.

6. Carl F. H. Henry, *Confessions of a Theologian: An Autobiography* (Waco, Tex.: Word, 1986).

7. Ramsey, *Who Speaks for the Churches?*

8. James DeForest Murch, *Cooperation Without Compromise. A History of the National Association of Evangelicals* (Grand Rapids, Mich.: Eerdmans, 1956).

9. Murch, *Cooperation Without Compromise*, pp. 210–243. See also the following by James DeForest Murch, "God's Word and the Church's Witness," *United Evangelical Action* 8 (Apr. 1, 1949): 13–16; "Spirit of Revival Marks Indianapolis Meeting," *United Evangelical Action* 9 (May 1, 1950): 5; "In the Pattern of Peaceful Coexistence," *United Evangelical Action* 15 (May 1, 1956): 9; "Trends in Protestantism," *United Evangelical Action* 17 (Mar. 1, 1958): 7.

10. Alexis de Tocqueville, *Democracy in America*, ed. J. P. Maier, trans. George Lawrence (Garden City, N.Y.: Anchor Books, 1969), pp. 513–517. Quoted in Robert Putnam, "Bowling Alone," *Journal of Democracy* 6 (Jan. 1995): 65–78.

11. Henri Desroche, *Jacob and the Angel: An Essay in Sociologies of Religion* (Amherst: University of Massachusetts Press, 1957), p. 37.

12. William Rehnquist, dissenting in *Wallace* v. *Jaffree* 105 S.Ct. 2479 (1985).

13. In many of his writings, James Madison discusses a "line of distinction" between civil and religious authorities. See, for example, *Federalist Papers* X and LI.

Chapter Five

1. Eric Hoffer, *The True Believer: Thoughts on the Nature of Mass Movements* (New York: HarperCollins, 1951), pp. 89–90.

The Author

Martin E. Marty, the Fairfax M. Cone Distinguished Service Professor Emeritus at the University of Chicago, directed the three-year Public Religion Project for the Pew Charitable Trusts. Author of more than fifty books and winner of the National Book Award for *Righteous Empire*, Marty coedited five volumes for the Fundamentalism Project. He has received the National Humanities Medal and is in the first class of fellows of the American Academy of Political and Social Sciences. An ordained minister, Marty served for a decade as a Lutheran pastor before joining the University of Chicago faculty, where he taught for thirty-five years.

Jonathan Moore is a Ph.D. candidate in the history of Christianity at the University of Chicago Divinity School. His current research examines evangelicalism and church-state conflicts in twentieth-century America.

About the Public Religion Project

This book is a product of Public Religion Project–sponsored conversations on public religion and politics and government. The Public Religion Project, a three-year endeavor (1996–1999) funded by the Pew Charitable Trusts and hosted by the University of Chicago, held these conversations as part of its assignment to "promote efforts to bring to light and interpret the forces of faith within a pluralistic society."

This charter called on the project to find ways to help ensure that religion in its many voices was well represented in North American public life; to bring to the fore often neglected resources for healing of body, mind, spirit, and public life that religion manifests; to work to clarify the roles of religion in public spheres by engaging various expressions of faith, even those that are repressive or destructive; and to lift up situations in which dialogue, mutual respect, and the search for common values and solutions have successfully proceeded.

In these pursuits, the project did not line up with partisans in "culture wars" or ideological conflicts. Certainly, the project was "pro-publicness," contending that American society is better off when it is aware of the religious forces and voices, and thus it worked to enhance this concept of "public" religion while honoring the private and communal energizing sources and outlets of people of faith.

In its undertakings, the project considered ten zones of public life where forces of faith are at work. One of these was government and politics. In hosting the series of conversations on this topic, the project invited politicians, the politically active, and scholars of politics and government—all with a keen interest in religion—to the table. This book reflects the voices and concerns heard around that table.

I've often compared the project's work to that of atomic accelerators or jet propulsion laboratories: it took objects, events, energies, and forces already extant and active and set out to propel them into new areas. We hope this conversation, begun around our table and now continued with you, will be part of that dynamic.

Index